Dedicated to my father, in loving memory

Calm Your Mind in 5 Weeks

How to Reduce Anxiety Naturally

Jacqueline Brandes

"By changing nothing, nothing changes."

- Tony Robbins

DISCLAIMER

The purpose of this book is to provide information, dietary suggestions and practices for people suffering from anxiety.

This book is <u>not</u> intended to offer any medical advice.

The dietary changes and suggestions, breathing techniques and yoga practices in this book are <u>not</u> a substitute for proper medical care. They are meant to work in conjunctions with your current treatment.

If you are currently receiving treatment for anxiety, please consult your doctor or therapist before applying the dietary changes and doing the practices in this book to ensure that they don't interfere with your treatment.

It is always advisable to consult your doctor/health practitioner before starting any new diet or exercise program.

Do <u>not</u> stop taking your prescribed anti-anxiety medication (antidepressants) because this may result in worsening symptoms. Talk to your doctor first if you ever wish to reduce your anti-anxiety medication.

Please see your health practitioner if you feel that anxiety is significantly affecting your daily life.

Whilst the advice and information in this book has been thoroughly researched and carefully put together, the author cannot accept liability for any resulting injury, damage or loss to persons or property, however it may arise.

CONTENTS

ACKNOWLEDGMENTS

Many thanks to my partner Shane. Without your loving support and encouragement this would have not been possible. Thank you also for being such a great yoga pose photographer.

I also want to thank my proofreader and editor Therese Barber and book cover designer Nada Orlic.

INTRODUCTION

If you are looking for an anxiety-reducing program that is completely natural, based on diet and mind-calming exercises and which won't interfere with your anxiety medication (if you are taking any), then this program is 100% right for you.

This program has been specifically designed for people suffering from anxiety. However it is also great for people who get stressed easily or live a stressful and demanding life.

"Calm Your Mind in 5 Weeks" will guide you through the process of changing/adjusting your diet gradually by adding more and more anxiety-reducing foods each week and eliminating foods that are known to spike anxiety. In the first three weeks, you will also learn short breathing and meditation practices that you can easily incorporate into each day. Additionally, Week 4 introduces a yoga practice to further the progress of calming your mind.

Because the diet changes are gradual and the practices are short and easy, you won't feel overwhelmed. You are encouraged to follow the recommended weekly plan in order to get the most out of this program but if for some reason you aren't able to do a certain practice on one of the days, don't beat yourself up about it. Instead stay positive and continue on the next day. At the same time, you are more than welcome to do the breathing/meditation and yoga practices as often as you like. They won't harm you, on the contrary, they will make you progress faster and deepen your experience.

In this book you will learn in detail which foods are great anti-anxiety foods and why, as well as which foods you should avoid completely. You will also be given alternatives to the foods you'll be eliminating out of your diet. This book also contains a meal plan and recipes to give you some suggestions on how to incorporate those anxiety-fighting foods into your diet.

To summarise, you will gain a bucket load of knowledge which you will benefit from immensely. There may also be little "aha" moments as you read through the information. It is fascinating how much your food influences your feelings and therefore the well-known saying "You are what you eat" makes so much sense. Apart from our diet the use of breathing practices, meditation and specific mind-calming yoga exercises are also very powerful in tackling anxiety and have therefore been included in this program. In fact, there is a breathing technique that can stop panic attacks in their tracks.

Lifestyle changes are one of the keys in overcoming anxiety and you will be amazed how much these five weeks will transform you! Best of all is that over this period, these small changes will form into habits that you can easily maintain.

MY STORY

I suffered with anxiety for over 10 years. At times, it has only been mild chronic anxiety but there have been particularly tough times where I was suffering from moderate to high anxiety and panic attacks on a regular basis – which was very frightening and debilitating (as you probably know yourself). I just couldn't function properly anymore and felt constantly overwhelmed with even normal day-to-day life. The physical symptoms I experienced ranged from severe dizziness to headaches, chronic neck, shoulder and back pain. I went to see a lot of different doctors and specialists to get on top of my problems but unfortunately nothing really seemed to work. A couple of times I even ended up in the emergency room of a hospital due to a panic attack. At that point in time, I wasn't aware that it was "just" a panic attack that I was experiencing.

My worst experience was after the sudden and unexpected death of my father in 2006. I had just started a life in a new country (Australia), having emigrated from Germany. A year later I suffered from a very harsh and persistent influenza virus for months which I just couldn't shake. All of this combined on top of a high-pressure IT job. It was too much for my body and at that point anxiety took hold of me completely. I was suffering from anxiety on a daily basis.

At the beginning of 2009 I was made redundant from my corporate job and for a while felt that everything that I had worked for was slowly vanishing before my eyes. It took me some time to comprehend my situation but eventually I started to look at it in a positive way and began to see that moment as a turning-point in my life, maybe even the opportunity to completely re-invent myself.

My body has always been very sensitive to any medication, usually adversely reacting with a lot of side effects. It was because of this that I decided to explore other alternatives such as natural remedies and therapies. My quest led me to Chiropractors, Osteopaths, Physiotherapists, Kinesiologists and Acupuncturists. I also tried and experimented with countless herbal anti-anxiety remedies and foods.

After researching many different natural therapies and practices, I embarked on a training course to become a qualified Solomon Yogalates™ instructor, which is a blend of Yoga and Pilates and combines these two practices into a truly unique and uplifting workout routine. Throughout the study, I followed the routines myself and was astounded in the changes I saw, both physically and mentally. After becoming a certified Solomon Yogalates™ instructor, I completed further training in Iyengar Yoga and therapeutical aspects of yoga. I became very passionate about therapeutic yoga and soon began to study how specific yoga exercises can help to calm the mind and relieve anxiety.

Over the years, I've learned a lot about reducing anxiety naturally and I am excited and passionate about helping other people to overcome anxiety by sharing my knowledge.

WEEK 1

Week 1 is very important in setting the foundation for the following weeks. By the end of this first week you should start to notice some improvement in your anxiety levels. Ok, let's get started!

Your tasks for this week are:

- Adding foods that are high in magnesium
- Avoiding caffeine
- Avoiding alcohol
- Practicing 10 minutes of Belly Breathing each day

Tip: Be kind to yourself and allow a few days to adjust to the diet changes.

Task 1: Adding foods that are high in magnesium

Anxiety Reliever: Magnesium

Magnesium is involved with over 300 metabolic processes in our bodies and is often called the relaxation mineral because it relaxes the muscles, lowers stress levels and calms an overly excited nervous system. It is basically an antidote to stress.

Can you see how helpful and beneficial this mineral could be in overcoming anxiety?

But here is where it starts to become a bit challenging; stress depletes the body of magnesium. The more stressed you are, the greater the loss of magnesium. Low magnesium levels on the other hand make you more susceptible to stress and anxiety and exacerbate the symptoms. So, it is a bit like a vicious cycle.

Considering our busy, fast-paced, stress-filled lives, it is no big surprise that magnesium deficiency is in fact the most common mineral deficiency in the Western world.

Typical signs and symptoms of magnesium deficiency include:

- Anxiety
- Agitation
- Irritability
- Rapid breathing
- Irregular heart rhythm
- Muscle cramps, spasms and weakness
- Migraines and tension headaches
- Sensitivity to loud or sudden noises
- Poor concentration
- Poor memory
- Fatigue and lethargy
- Eye twitches
- Hand tremors

- High blood pressure
- Nausea
- Dizziness
- Confusion.

What this means is that the anxiety you are experiencing could potentially be caused by low magnesium levels – or low magnesium levels contribute to your anxiety. But keep in mind that it doesn't necessarily mean that you are deficient in magnesium if you are experiencing any of the above listed symptoms.

No matter what, it is still always a good idea to make sure you get enough magnesium in your diet, especially if you are suffering from chronic anxiety or stress. That is also the main reason why I chose to start off with adding foods that are high in magnesium in Week 1 of this program.

Apart from chronic stress, other contributing factors to magnesium deficiency are:

- Caffeine
- Alcohol
- Diet high in fat, sugar and salt
- Smoking
- Certain medications such as diuretics, antibiotics and cancer medications
- Certain diseases such as Crohn's disease and Coeliac disease.

It is always best to get magnesium from natural food sources. But of course, it is also possible and may be beneficial for some to supplement with magnesium especially if your magnesium levels are extremely low. Ask your healthcare professional for advice and recommended dosage.

Magnesium-rich foods

The following foods are high in magnesium:

- Almonds (preferably organic pesticide-free almonds)
- Avocados
- Bananas
- Dark chocolate/ raw cacao
- Dark leafy greens (e.g. spinach, kale or broccoli – preferably organic)
- Quinoa.

You should aim to include at least two of those foods into your daily diet.

There are, of course, more foods that contain magnesium but the ones listed above contain the most magnesium and therefore show the best results.

Try mixing two or more of those magnesium-rich foods in a meal for optimal results.

The meal plan and recipes at the back of this book give some ideas on how to incorporate those magnesium-rich foods into your daily diet. These are only suggestions, so you can be as creative as you wish.

Note: If you are using raw dark leafy greens in smoothies or juices, make sure you rotate between two different leafy greens per week (e.g. kale and spinach). All raw leafy greens contain a small amount of toxins (which is the plant's defence mechanism for predators) that can build up in the body, leading to negative side effects. This may only happen if the same type of green is consumed over a long period of time.

I, personally, like dark chocolate with almonds, green smoothies with spinach and banana as well as bananas on their own as snacks in between meals. A handful of almonds is also a great snack. As you can see, you don't need to change your diet that much in this first week – just include some of those snacks.

Quinoa

Quinoa is a nutrient-rich grain which not only contains magnesium, but also B vitamins, vitamin E, calcium, copper, iron, manganese, phosphorus, potassium and zinc. It is gluten-free and contains significantly more protein than other grains. There are three main varieties of this ancient grain – white, red and black quinoa. White quinoa has a mild, nutty flavour and can be used as an alternative to rice, couscous or other grains. Red and black quinoa has an earthier flavour, is crunchier and has a more fibrous texture than white quinoa.

Quinoa can be cooked in the same way as rice, meaning that it can also be cooked in a rice cooker. Serve it with vegetables, legumes or meat. It is also great in soups and salads, and can even be made into a porridge.

In their natural state, the Quinoa seeds are coated with bitter-tasting saponins which are usually rinsed off prior to packaging. But it is always best to rinse it again before use to get rid of any remaining traces of the saponins on the seeds. Please also check the package for specific preparation and cooking instructions.

Dark chocolate/raw cacao

Cacao is an excellent source of magnesium if not the number one source! Apart from its high levels of magnesium, chromium, iron and manganese, it is also rich in tryptophan, serotonin and phenylethylamines (PEAs). On top of that is also listed as the world's top antioxidant food. Tryptophan, serotonin and PEAs are mood enhancers and generate feelings of well-being.

Make sure you don't confuse cacao with cocoa! The spelling looks very similar but there is a difference between cacao and cocoa.

Raw cacao is made by cold-pressing unroasted cocoa beans which keeps all of the good nutrients in. Raw cacao is rich in minerals and in particular magnesium. Only raw cacao contains PEAs. Because PEAs are heat-sensitive, they are not present in conventional processed chocolate.

Cocoa powder on the other hand is raw cacao that has been roasted at high temperatures which lowers the overall nutritional value.

Conclusion: Raw cacao products which are made with cacao beans, nibs, powder or cacao butter are the ones that contain the most nutrients and therefore offer the most health benefits!

The easiest way to include raw cacao products into your diet is by blending raw cacao powder (preferably organic) into your favourite beverage (e.g. coconut water, teas or coffee). Dosage: Approximately one tablespoon of cacao powder per litre (or quart).

If you can't get your hands on raw cacao powder or are after a quick and easy magnesium-rich snack, dark chocolate that contains at least 70 percent cocoa is a good option. If you can tolerate the bitter taste (it may take some time to get used to it), dark chocolate with 75 to 85 percent cocoa is ideal. The higher the percentage of cocoa, the more health benefits it offers. Compared to milk chocolate, dark chocolate has a much higher cocoa content and contains more magnesium and less sugar. Dark chocolate is rich in antioxidants and has a higher nutritional value than milk chocolate and is therefore the better option. But don't overindulge in dark chocolate either as it does contain sugar and of course calories.

Also, more and more there are raw chocolate bars and other raw chocolate snacks (e.g. raw chocolate/cacao goodie balls) available in health food stores as well as some supermarkets.

Note: Cacao/ chocolate products do contain a small amount of caffeine but this is nothing to worry about. It won't make you jittery or keep you up at night as the caffeine content in cacao products is only a fraction of the caffeine present in conventional coffee.

Tip: Another great way to increase the magnesium levels in your body is to take a bath with Epsom salts. Epsom salts are rich in magnesium and sulfate. When dissolved in warm water, Epsom salt is absorbed through the skin and thereby replenishes the magnesium levels in the body. A bath with Epsom salts relaxes the nervous system as well as sore muscles. It also eliminates toxins from the body. Add about a cup of Epsom salts to your bath water. You can also add a few drops of lavender essential oil which helps to calm restlessness. Epsom salts can be found in most supermarkets, chemists as well as health food stores.

Task 2: Avoiding caffeine

Caffeine is the most widely consumed psychoactive drug in the world. It can typically be found in coffee, black tea, green tea, some soft drinks (such as cola) and energy drinks as well as various foods (e.g. chocolate, foods containing cocoa, etc.).

Avoiding caffeine may be tough for some of you but you will benefit from avoiding it as much as possible as this is one of the major contributors to anxiety. In fact, most anxiety sufferers are sensitive to caffeine.

Anxiety Stimulant: Caffeine

Caffeine acts as a stimulant drug that affects the central nervous system, the heart and digestive secretions. It activates the "fight or flight response" in the body which makes you not only alert but also raises your blood pressure, your heart pumps faster and your body releases stress hormones.

People suffering from panic attacks know very well what the "fight or flight response" does to the body and mind and how uncomfortable, frightening and debilitating it can be. The "fight or flight response" is a physiological reaction that occurs in response to a perceived harmful event, attack or threat to our survival and prepares the body to "fight" or "flee". It increases the heart rate, blood pressure and breathing rate and makes you feel as if you were experiencing a life-threatening event.

This is a handy response to have if you are running from a pack of thugs. But it is less useful, and in fact detrimental to our health, to have when we're sitting still at the computer, driving the kids to school or doing the grocery shopping. Because caffeine activates this response, it can cause the body to become exhausted by over-stimulating the release of stress hormones which ultimately burns your body out.

Depending on the caffeine dose as well as the time of consumption, it can lead to restlessness, irritability, anxiety and insomnia.

Caffeine has also been shown to inhibit levels of serotonin, the "feel good" hormone, in the brain which can make you feel irritable and anxious.

Caffeine also depletes the body of magnesium as well as other important minerals such as calcium and potassium. Magnesium is a very important mineral as you have just learned.

There are other known side effects caused by caffeine consumption, and there are also some reported health benefits, particularly in relation to illnesses such as Alzheimer's disease, depression and even some cancers. But the focus of this book and program is on anxiety and not a full debate on the merits or otherwise of caffeine, so I won't go into any more detail. Suffice to say, caffeine is not helping anxiety sufferers.

Eliminating caffeine from your diet may not be an easy task because over time the body forms a dependency on it. The best way to go about eliminating it is doing it gradually. For example, if you normally drink two cups of coffee per day, reduce it to one or ask for a half-strength coffee instead of a full-strength one. And then gradually get to a point where you can eliminate caffeine completely.

In the first few days, you may experience some caffeine withdrawal symptoms such as headaches, irritability, lack of concentration and sleepiness. This is perfectly normal and will subside after those first few days. But this may only happen if your body is used to a daily dose of caffeine.

Consider seeking professional help if you feel like you are struggling too much with this task. Acupuncture, for example, greatly helps to overcome addictions and rebalance hormones.

Alternatives to caffeinated drinks

Herbal teas

Herbal teas are excellent alternatives to caffeinated drinks. They not only taste great, but also have many health benefits. All of the herbal teas listed here have calming, anxiety-relieving properties and therefore are great choices for anxiety sufferers. I suggest you try them all over time and find out which ones you like most and work best for you.

Black teas contain caffeine, so stay clear of those. Even though black teas don't contain as much caffeine as coffee, it can still be enough to trigger anxiety.

Tip: Always check the label of your herbal tea to ensure it is not just black tea infused with herbs or fruit.

Warning/Caution: Some herbal teas may interact with certain medications. It is advisable to talk to your doctor/ health practitioner prior to consumption.

Peppermint tea

Peppermint tea is a very refreshing and revitalising drink and a great alternative to coffee. The aroma of peppermint tea is known to make you alert and focused without aggravating anxiety or making you nervous and jittery. At the same time it acts as a muscle relaxant with stomach settling properties. It is therefore excellent if your stomach feels a bit stirred up from anxious feelings.

Green tea

Green tea is full of antioxidants and has a huge list of health benefits including anti-anxiety properties. The amino acid L-theanine found in green tea promotes relaxation and is known to reduce mental and physical stress. At the same time, it boosts your mental focus, making you more alert without any of the coffee jitters.

But keep in mind that green tea *does* contain caffeine. The caffeine content in green tea is much lower than in coffee and usually lower than in black tea. While the L-theanine somewhat neutralises the effects of caffeine, it can still be enough to aggravate anxiety if you are very sensitive to caffeine. I prefer drinking decaffeinated green tea. You still get the same benefits with much less caffeine than caffeinated green teas. Yes, even decaffeinated green teas contain a very small amount of caffeine but this is hardly noticeable.

Green tea blends, such as a 50-50 blend of lemongrass and green tea, mint and green tea or fruit and green tea, contain about half the caffeine of normal, unblended green tea.

Did you know that brewing green tea incorrectly can increase the level of caffeine? To brew green tea correctly, don't use boiling water, instead use simmering water and brew for 30 seconds to four minutes. Also, always check the brewing instructions on the tea bag or box.

Chamomile tea

Chamomile tea is very soothing for the nervous system. It is not only perfect during stressful times but also a great remedy for stomach aches as it relaxes the muscles and lining of the intestines. I like drinking chamomile tea in the evening as it helps me to unwind and makes me fall asleep easier.

Lemon Balm/ Melissa tea

Lemon balm (Melissa Officinalis) tea, also known as Melissa tea is another great anxiety fighter. Lemon balm is widely used to treat anxiety, stress and insomnia. It is a mild sedative which has a very pleasant calming effect that may help to induce sleep. But at the same time, it is also known for uplifting the mood and assisting in gaining mental clarity and improving concentration.

Lavender tea

Lavender tea with its mild floral scent is well-known for its calming, nervous-tension and muscle-spasm relieving properties. The scent of lavender alone helps to ease anxiety and insomnia. Lavender tea is therefore a great bedtime tea. Sometimes other herbal teas such as chamomile or peppermint tea are blended with lavender. They are not only delicious but also complement each other perfectly as they have similar calming, anxiety-relieving properties.

Rooibos tea

Rooibos tea is also caffeine free and full of minerals that are vital to our health, such as magnesium, calcium, manganese and iron. Because of its magnesium content, rooibos tea helps you to feel calm and relaxed. This tea is also great before bedtime as it promotes a restful sleep.

Passionflower tea

Passionflower (Passiflora incarnata) tea has nerve calming/sedative and muscle spasm relieving effects and is often used to promote restful sleep. It is also used as a remedy for nervous, menopausal and premenstrual tension, irritability and nervousness, palpitations, irregular heartbeat, tension headaches, high blood pressure and gastrointestinal upset related to anxiety or nervousness. Passionflower tea is often blended with other relaxing herbs, such as Valerian, Chamomile, Lemon Balm, Skullcap and St. John's Wort.

Hawthorn tea

Hawthorn tea has a slightly sour/tart and bitter taste. It helps to ease tension, treat chest tightness and heart palpitations, and calms the nerves without inducing sleep. This makes it a great daytime tea. It is also often used as a heart tonic as it is believed to improve cardiovascular health and lower blood pressure. This tea is packed with antioxidants, high in vitamin C and contains small amounts of vitamin A, some B vitamins, potassium and magnesium.

Fruit teas

Fruit teas are delicious and great for summer. They are infusions of fruit extract or fruit juice and are packed with vitamins, minerals and antioxidants. Pure fruit teas don't contain any caffeine. Make sure you stay clear of fruit-infused black teas as they contain caffeine. It is always best to check the ingredients on the back of the package. And yes, it has happened to me a few times that I picked up a fruit infused black tea instead of a pure fruit tea because the label made it sound like a pure fruit tea.

Decaffeinated coffee

If you prefer the taste of coffee, try decaffeinated coffee. You still get the coffee taste but without the buzz. But keep in mind that even decaffeinated coffee can contain a very small amount of caffeine but it is so minor that you probably won't even notice it. I, personally, am very sensitive to caffeine but have no problems with decaffeinated coffee.

Caffeine-free coffee

The biggest difference between decaffeinated coffee and caffeine-free coffee is that caffeine-free coffee is not made out of coffee beans and therefore is truly caffeine-free.

Spelt coffee, for example, is prepared by roasting the spelt grains which creates a pleasant roasted flavour, similar to normal instant coffee.

Dandelion coffee (also called dandelion tea) is a herbal tea that is also often used as a coffee substitute. It is made from the roasted root of the dandelion plant making it look and taste like coffee. Sometimes dandelion tea is blended with roasted chicory root.

Another caffeine-free herbal coffee alternative is ***Teeccino*** which is a blend of herbs, grains, fruits and nuts that are roasted and ground. Like the other caffeine-free coffee alternatives, it imitates the taste of coffee. It also provides a gentle, natural energy boost.

These are just a few examples for caffeine-free coffee alternatives which you may want to try if you are a coffee-lover and can't go without the coffee taste.

Water

Water (spring, mineral or filtered water) is always a good choice, especially when you are on the go. It is easily available and great for hydrating your body. You can mix it with some fruit juice, if you don't like the taste of just water. Note: Fruit juices on their own are usually high in sugar and therefore shouldn't be consumed excessively. You will learn more about sugar and why you should reduce/limit its consumption in Week 2.

Tip: Make sure you hydrate your body properly throughout the day as dehydration can contribute to anxiety. Drink at least eight 8-ounce glasses (approximately 1.9 litres) of fluid a day.

Task 3: Avoiding alcohol

There are a few reasons why alcohol should be avoided when dealing with anxiety. Number one is that it depletes the body of magnesium which is so important in fighting stress and anxiety as we have previously discussed. Alcohol itself is actually an anxiety stimulant!

It is advisable to avoid alcohol completely during this program but if that is not possible for you, try to reduce your alcohol intake to the minimum, such as 1-2 glasses of wine on a special occasion.

Anxiety Stimulant: Alcohol

You may believe that drinking alcohol reduces anxiety because it tends to relax you but this is only half true. In fact, consuming alcohol can actually trigger anxiety.

Let's have a closer look at this.

Alcohol reduces the magnesium levels in your body and, as we have learnt before, magnesium deficiency can cause anxiety.

Alcohol also causes your body to release adrenalin which can then lead to typical anxiety symptoms such as a faster heart rate.

Furthermore, alcohol consumption causes a drop in blood sugars and dehydrates the body which can all be triggers for anxiety. Fluctuating blood sugar levels can produce symptoms of confusion, dizziness, nervousness and restlessness. Typical symptoms of dehydration are nausea, fatigue and muscle weakness which can make you become anxious.

It is true that alcohol tends to relax you to start with but this is only short term. Often you will feel more agitated a bit later. Alcohol is a central nervous system depressant which depresses arousal and stimulation by lowering neurotransmission levels in the brain. This will make you feel more relaxed to begin with. But alcohol goes on to also lower the levels of the neurotransmitter serotonin in your brain, the "feel-good" hormone.

This neurotransmitter is responsible for regulating your mood. Once serotonin is deficient, you are likely to experience symptoms such as anxiety, negative thoughts, excessive worrying, agitation, mood swings and inability to fall or stay asleep – all of which are very common after-effects of alcohol consumption.

As you can see, anxiety and alcohol don't mix very well and therefore it should definitely be avoided.

Task 4: Practice: Belly Breathing

Over the first three weeks of this program, I want to teach you three short practices that are easy, anxiety-reducing techniques. They only require 10 minutes of your time and ideally you will be doing these on a daily basis.

This week, we're getting you started with a short breathing practice which is called Belly Breathing. But before I get to that, I want to show you the important role breath plays in our emotional well-being and how simple breathing exercises can relieve anxiety and stress. There is even a breathing technique that can stop a panic attack in its tracks.

Breathing and Anxiety – The power of your breath

The breath is an important indicator of a person's emotional and mental state. If our breath is slow and deep, we feel calm and relaxed. Rapid, shallow breathing on the other hand makes us feel anxious and stressed. It is quite interesting to know that shallow breathing can trigger anxiety but anxiety also causes shallow breathing. This shows us that our breathing and emotional/mental state are interconnected.

Breathing is regulated by the autonomic, or involuntary, nervous system which means we don't have to consciously initiate the breath, it automatically happens. But the breath is also controlled by the voluntary nervous system which means we can breathe intentionally. In fact, we are the only creature on this planet that can breathe either consciously or unconsciously. Knowing this gives anxiety sufferers incredible power. If we change our breathing pattern and rate consciously to deeper and slower breaths, we can trigger the relaxation response in the body – meaning we will feel calmer, more relaxed and less anxious. By simply changing the way we breathe, we can basically reverse the body's stress response and alter our emotional and mental state. How good is that!?

I'll repeat that again because it is so important:

By consciously changing how we breathe, we can change how we feel.

Let's do a short breathing test to find out more about your breathing

"Check in with your breath" – A short breathing test

This test is just to check into your breathing habits and may help you understand the following paragraphs better.

1. Sit up straight in a chair with your feet flat on the floor.
2. Place one hand on your chest and the other hand on your belly.
3. Take a few slow, deep breaths and notice the movement of your hands. Which hand moves the most as you breathe in? Is it the hand on your chest or your belly?
   If you are breathing into both: Where does the breathing primarily happen? Where is it initiated? Which movement is bigger – the movement in the chest or the movement in the belly?

If you were breathing primarily into your chest, then you are a chest breather. Read more about it in the paragraph "Chest breathing - The anxious breath".

If you were breathing primarily into your belly, then you are a belly or diaphragmatic breather. Read more about it in the paragraph "Diaphragmatic breathing - The relaxing breath".

Note: You can do this short breathing test any time to check into your breathing habits and emotional wellbeing.

Chest breathing - The anxious breath

Chest breathing is often associated with anxiety as it tends to be rapid and shallow. In fact, anxiety is more frequently associated with chest breathing as opposed to diaphragmatic breathing if it is a person's primary breathing pattern.

Chest breathing is less efficient than normal diaphragmatic breathing. It creates more tension in the chest as well as the whole body. It comes to the fore during strenuous exercise to provide the body with the large amounts of oxygen it needs.

During a threatening or stressful situation when the "fight-or-flight" response kicks in, the body automatically switches to chest breathing due to its higher oxygen requirements. The body is basically preparing to fight or flee and therefore requires more oxygen to power the muscles. This causes the breath to become rapid and shallow. But when the body's "fight-or-flight" preparation doesn't result in physical activity to use up the high oxygen levels, it can lead to a form of hyperventilation.

During hyperventilation, the decrease of carbon dioxide in the blood can cause physical symptoms such as light-headedness, shortness of breath, dizziness, numbness or tingling in the hands or feet, nausea, chest pain and overall weakness in the body. It may even feel like you are about to faint. As scary as this is when you experience it, the good news is that by changing your breathing you can actually reverse these symptoms (see **Breathing through a panic attack**).

Some people develop a habit of chest breathing, even when they are not stressed or anxious. Chronic chest breathing can lead to a chronic anxious state in which even minor stressors can trigger an acute "fight-or-flight" reaction.

Also, tension in the lower abdomen as a result of feelings such as fear or aggression, or simply caused by pulling in the abdominals in order to look "thinner" can stiffen the diaphragm which will result in chest breathing.

Diaphragmatic breathing - The relaxing breath

Diaphragmatic breathing is deeper and slower than chest breathing and is optimal for our well-being. It is the body's normal breathing pattern during times of low physical activity.

A perfect example of diaphragmatic breathing can be witnessed when watching sleeping babies. Lying on their backs, their bellies rise and fall softly with every breath. For most of us when we are relaxed or resting, in particular during deep sleep, our breathing occurs primarily in the belly. This utilises the diaphragm which sits just beneath your rib cage. By consciously practicing this breathing technique, we can trigger the relaxation response in our body, releasing tension and promoting a sense of tranquillity. This breathing technique is called Belly Breathing and it is the first breathing technique you will learn in this program.

Interesting fact: You can't breathe deeply and be anxious at the same time. Give it a try if you don't believe it!

Belly Breathing instructions

For people with mild anxiety/stress I suggest practicing Belly Breathing for 10 minutes daily.

Those people with moderate anxiety/stress, practice Belly Breathing twice daily for 10 minutes (for example: 10 minutes in the morning and 10 minutes in the evening).

If you do this practice at the same time each day it may make it easier for you to remember and help get you into the habit faster.

Find a quiet place where you won't be disturbed.

1. Lie on your back - either on a blanket or yoga mat on the floor, or even in bed - with your knees bent and your feet on the floor/bed.
2. Place both hands on your lower belly.
3. Close your eyes.

4.   Inhale and breathe into the belly. Feel the belly rise. Inflate the belly gently. Do not apply force.

5.   Exhale and let the belly relax fully. Feel the belly fall.

6.   Continue for about 10 minutes, concentrating completely on your belly and your breathing. Take slow, deep and even breaths. Notice how calming and soothing this practice is.

Once you are finished, take some time and don't jump up straight away. Roll onto your right side and stay there for a minute or two. Then slowly push yourself up to sitting and then standing. The reason for this is that your nervous system is very calm and relaxed after this practice. Jumping up too quickly can agitate your nervous system which is counterproductive to the purpose of this exercise.

Tip: Try doing this breathing exercise during your most anxious times as this will make you feel so much calmer afterwards.

Here are two more, simple breathing techniques that are very useful at times when you are feeling anxious or when you are experiencing a panic attack:

Breathing when you feel anxious

Breathe in through the nose to a count of four and then out through the mouth to a count of five. Repeat this four times.

This little breathing routine will initiate the relaxation response in your body.

Breathing through a panic attack

When experiencing a panic attack, follow these steps to stop hyperventilating and reverse the physical symptoms associated with it:

1. Take a deep breath in and hold it for about 20 seconds or so before exhaling.
2. The aim now is to slow your breathing rate down to about 10 seconds for a full breath. Breathe in while counting to 5 in your head and breathe out counting to 5 again. Continue doing this for the next 2 minutes.

This little breathing practice slows down the rapid, shallow breathing that is associated with panic attacks. It is very simple and easy and yet so powerful.

Summary of Week 1

- Eat foods that are high in magnesium: almonds, avocados, bananas, dark chocolate/ raw cacao, dark leafy greens (spinach, kale, broccoli), quinoa
- Avoid caffeine: substitute coffee with herbal teas
- Avoid alcohol
- Practice 10 minutes of Belly Breathing daily

Action: Check out the meal plan as well as the recipes for Week 1 at the back of this book and start planning your week ahead.

This week's meal plan is intended to give you some suggestions and ideas on how to incorporate magnesium-rich foods into your diet.

Action: List all of your actions/ goals for Week 1.

For example:
To increase my magnesium intake I will eat …
I will substitute my cup of coffee with …
I will do 10 minutes of Belly Breathing at … each day.

My Action Plan – Week 1

✓	
✓	
✓	
✓	
✓	
✓	
✓	
✓	
✓	
✓	

Action: Practice some Belly Breathing right now before reading on!

WEEK 2

Well done, you have completed your first week of this journey to a calmer YOU. You may notice less anxiety and stress already but this is just the start of it. It will get even better! So, let's tackle Week 2 of this program.

Your tasks for this week are:

- Continue to apply dietary changes from Week 1
- Add foods that are rich in omega-3 fatty acids
- Reduce sugar and avoid all artificial sweeteners
- Practice 10 minutes of Meditation each day

Task 1: Applying dietary changes from Week 1

Your first task of this second week is to keep going with the dietary changes from Week 1. So, keep consuming magnesium-rich foods, avoid caffeine and alcohol.

Task 2: Adding foods that are rich in omega-3 fatty acids

Anxiety Reliever: Omega-3 fatty acids

Omega-3 fatty acids are polyunsaturated fatty acids that are essential for our health. They cannot be produced by our own bodies and therefore can only be obtained from our diet. They play an important role in brain health as they are highly concentrated in the brain and help to improve its blood flow. A diet rich in omega-3 fatty acids has been proven to lower the body's stress response and levels of cortisol, the stress hormone. Some studies even demonstrate antidepressant properties.

Omega-3-fatty-acid-rich foods

Omega-3 fatty acids can be obtained from vegetables or fish and are commonly found in fish and plant oils.

Listed below are some foods that are rich in omega-3 fatty acids:

- Oily fish, such as salmon, sardines, tuna, mackerel or trout
- Chia Seeds
- Walnuts
- Spirulina - also contains magnesium (Week 1), tryptophan (Week 3) and is rich in B vitamins (Week 4)
- Flaxseed/linseed and its oil
- Olive oil.

This week we are aiming to include at least one of those foods into your daily diet. But do not eat more than two fish meals per week because of the high levels of mercury that some fish can contain. Mercury is a poison that interferes with the brain and nervous system and may cause developmental delays in developing foetuses and young children. Some tuna can contain higher levels of mercury and therefore should be eaten in moderation. It is best to stick to the smaller oily fish like salmon, sardines, mackerel and trout as they contain less mercury.

You can take a daily dose of fish oil or krill oil supplements, but keep in mind that it is always best to obtain omega-3 fatty acids from natural sources. Also, omega-3 fatty acid supplements can interfere with some medications such as blood thinning and diabetes medications, so check with your doctor if these supplements are safe for you to use.

Spirulina

Spirulina is a blue-green freshwater microalgae and is considered a "superfood" because of its high nutrient density.

Spirulina is not only rich in omega-3 fatty acids, but also rich in B vitamins and contains a wide range of minerals including magnesium, calcium, potassium, iron, etc. It is a complete protein source, including the amino acid tryptophan which is important for serotonin production.

Spirulina powder can easily be added to smoothies, fresh juices and raw cacao treats. It can even be sprinkled on top of salads.

Try adding Spirulina powder to the green smoothie recipe in this book. Start off with only ½ teaspoon and gradually increase the dosage to 1 teaspoon of Spirulina powder per day. [The "beginner" dose is up to 1 teaspoon (3-5 grams) per day. The "normal" dose for an adult is 1-2 teaspoons per day (6-10 grams).]

You can purchase Spirulina powder from health food stores as well as online. I have also seen it in some supermarkets. Make sure you buy organic Spirulina powder or clean Spirulina powder, the latter being completely free from heavy metals and foreign contaminants of any kind.

Warning: People with an algae/seaweed, shellfish, seafood or iodine allergy should avoid Spirulina. If you suffer from the rare disease phenylketonuria (PKU), you should also avoid Spirulina. Also, avoid taking Spirulina if you have an autoimmune disease such as rheumatoid arthritis, multiple sclerosis or lupus as Spirulina may exacerbate the symptoms associated with those conditions.

Some medical professionals advise that Spirulina should not be taken by children, pregnant or breastfeeding women.

Because Spirulina is a detoxifying agent, you may experience slight detoxification symptoms such as stomach ache, nausea, constipation, diarrhea, slight fever, headache or itchy skin. If this happens, lower the dosage and then slowly increase it up to 1 teaspoon per day.

Chia Seeds

Apart from being rich in omega-3 fatty acids, chia seeds are a good source of B vitamins, rich in antioxidants and contain calcium, potassium, magnesium, iron and phosphorous.

They have a mild, nutty flavour and come in different forms such as whole seeds (black or white), chia bran, ground chia and chia seed oil.

You can add them to breakfast cereals/muesli, smoothies (add about 1 tbsp. of chia seeds) or baked goods. They can also be sprinkled on yogurt, salads or rice dishes.

When you add liquid to chia seeds, they absorb it and turn into a gelatin-like substance. That way, they can be made into a healthy pudding or used to thicken soups and sauces.

They can even be used as an egg substitute in recipes. Combine 1 tablespoon of ground chia seeds with 3 tablespoons of water per egg in baked recipes.

Flaxseed/linseed

Flaxseed, also called linseed, is high in omega-3 fatty acids, rich in antioxidants, B vitamins as well as fibre.

Ground flaxseeds can be added to cereals, smoothies, yogurt, salads, baked breads and muffins. Start off by adding 1 tablespoon of ground flaxseeds per day. You can gradually increase the dosage up to 2-4 tablespoons per day. As flaxseeds are high in fibre, your digestive system may need some time to adjust to it.

Ground flaxseeds tend to go rancid quickly, therefore it is best to store them in an airtight container in the refrigerator or freezer.

You can also buy whole flaxseeds and use a coffee bean grinder or blender to grind them up as you need them.

Choose organic flaxseeds to avoid GMO varieties.

Task 3: Reducing sugar and avoiding all artificial sweeteners

This week, I am asking you to reduce sugar and avoid all artificial sweeteners. While I want you to avoid all artificial sweeteners completely as they have been proven to be harmful to your health (even more so than sugar), I suggest that you try to reduce the amount of sugar you are consuming and/or try some of the sugar alternatives (→ see **Alternatives to sugar and artificial sweeteners**).

Anxiety Stimulant: Sugar

Sugar, in particular processed sugars, are now known to contribute to a range of health problems, and studies show links with dietary diseases such as obesity and type 2 diabetes, but what you may not be aware of is that sugar can also affect your mental health.

Consuming sugar will at first cause a spike, followed by a fast drop in your blood sugar levels. When this happens the hormones adrenaline and cortisol are released, which can accentuate the symptoms of mood disorders such as depression and anxiety. In fact, a high-sugar diet may actually contribute to your anxiety by worsening the symptoms or causing feelings that trigger anxiety attacks.

You may also not be aware of the fact that sugar can cause blurry vision, difficulty thinking and fatigue which you may wrongly interpret as the first signs of a panic attack. The fear of an oncoming panic attack can then trigger anxiety and even an actual panic attack.

Another interesting thing to know about sugar is that it causes inflammation in the gut, body and brain which triggers an inflammation-immune chain reaction response, which also triggers an anxiety response.

Sugar and anxiety don't go well together. It is therefore best for anxiety sufferers to limit their sugar intake.

Sarah Wilson, author of the book "I Quit Sugar" recommends eating products with less than six grams of sugar per 100 grams or 100 millilitres.

In dairy products, the first 4.7 grams of sugar per 100 grams listed will be lactose – anything above that is added sugar.

It can be hard to avoid sugar as it is often added in foods we don't even consider as sugar foods, such as bread, salad dressings, potato chips, tinned vegetables, tomato and other sauces. In fact, sugar is hidden in most processed foods and therefore it is always a good idea to check the ingredients list on the products you are intending to buy.

The ingredients are always listed in order of the amount used in the product. Sometimes, especially when the product contains a large amount of sugar, it can be disguised in the ingredients by listing different kinds of sugar lower in the ingredients list.

The most common sources of sugar found on food labels are:

- Brown sugar
- Corn sweetener
- Corn syrup (high-fructose corn syrup)
- Dextrose
- Fructose
- Fruit-juice concentrate
- Glucose
- Inverted or invert sugar syrup
- Lactose
- Maltose
- Malt syrup
- Raw sugar
- Sucrose
- Syrup.

Another trick is to avoid the centre aisles in your supermarket which typically host the processed foods. This technique is called "shopping the outside" as fresh, unprocessed (or at least less processed) foods tend to be positioned around the outer walls of your supermarket.

Tip: Avoid buying low-fat products because the fat content is typically replaced with sugar.

Since a dramatic sugar spike and subsequent drop in blood sugar can cause anxiety symptoms such as shaking and tension, it is better to eat foods that provide a slow and steady rise in blood sugar levels. These are called low glycaemic foods or low-GI foods and include whole grains, proteins, vegetables and fruit.

It is also important to keep your blood sugar levels steady throughout the day as low blood sugar can contribute to anxiety as well. Low blood sugar levels cause the body to produce adrenaline to prevent fainting. The adrenaline then leads to anxiety symptoms such as heart racing and trembling. So, when you haven't eaten for a while and anxious feelings suddenly appear out of nowhere, this may be due to low blood sugar. In this case, try to eat a healthy snack such as a handful of almonds or walnuts, or a piece of dark chocolate and avoid sugary foods as well as simple carbohydrates (e.g. white wheat flour products). This will slowly raise your blood sugar levels and those feelings will most likely disappear within a short amount of time. To prevent blood sugar levels from dropping too low, you should eat small, frequent meals throughout your day (approximately every three to four hours).

How to beat sugar cravings

I understand that it may be difficult to avoid sugary foods at times as sometimes we just crave them.

Here are a few tips on how to curb your sugar cravings:

1. Try eating a teaspoon of virgin coconut oil (you can also blend it into your smoothie) or some nuts instead of a sweet snack. As you usually crave sugary foods when you are hungry, eating fats and/or proteins will fuel your energy reserves properly and you won't crave sweets.
2. Use cinnamon for sweetening your tea, porridge (oatmeal) or cereal. Cinnamon helps to balance blood sugar levels and hence stops sugar cravings.

3. Replace sweets with fruits. Although fruits do contain sugars, they are digested differently than normal table sugar. Apart from vitamins, minerals and enzymes, they also contain fibre which slows the absorption of the sugars, so you won't get the blood sugar spike followed by the crash.

4. Eat 1-2 squares of dark chocolate (70% cocoa or higher) or 1-2 teaspoons of unsweetened cacao or cocoa powder. Cocoa, which is the dominant ingredient in dark chocolate, elevates both dopamine and serotonin levels. This promotes happy feelings and reduces sugar cravings. It is interesting to note that if your dopamine and serotonin levels are low you will crave sugary foods.

5. Some women crave chocolate around the time of their periods. This may indicate that you are low on magnesium. Eat magnesium-rich foods such as a handful of almonds or some dark chocolate (70% cocoa or higher) to curb your cravings.

6. Don't eat sweets until after 3 pm. Eating sweets in the morning or early afternoon stimulates sweet cravings throughout the day.

7. Avoid artificial sweeteners as they cause intense cravings for sweets.

8. Don't skip meals. Instead eat small, frequent meals to keep your blood sugar levels stable and eliminate your body's need for a quick sugar fix. Try having 5 smaller meals a day, including breakfast, mid-morning snack, lunch, mid-afternoon snack and dinner.

Anxiety Stimulant: Artificial sweeteners

Artificial sweeteners are synthetic sugar substitutes and are known as intense sweeteners because they are many times sweeter than regular sugar. They are often used to substitute sugar in "weight loss" foods because they don't contain any calories and are claimed to not affect blood sugar levels.

However, artificial sweeteners play a trick on the body which can aggravate anxiety. When consuming an artificial sweetener the body reacts as if it is actual sugar and tries to store glucose which isn't there. This process of looking for and not finding glucose then stimulates the hunger for sugar and triggers a stress response in the body which can cause heart palpitations, headaches and muscle cramps.

Artificial sweeteners can also have neurotoxic effects on the body which can lead to, or make you prone to, anxiety attacks, depression, headaches, Tachycardia/heart palpitations, dizziness, seizures and tremors as well as abdominal pain, fatigue and physical weakness.

Aspartame appears to be the most controversial of the artificial sweeteners and has caused and still is causing a lot of debate about artificial sweeteners. A number of studies show that aspartame consumption can lead to excess levels of phenylalanine (an amino acid that is safe in small doses) which causes the levels of serotonin in the brain to decrease and can lead to anxiety, panic attacks, depression, insomnia, mood swings, hallucinations and even suicidal attempts.

I think those are enough good reasons to cut out artificial sweeteners from your diet once and for all.

Widely used artificial sweeteners include:

- **Acesulfame potassium** (brand names: Sunett, Sweet One)
- **Aspartame** (brand names: NutraSweet, Equal, Equal-Measure, Spoonful, Naturataste, Canderel, Benevia, etc.). Also known under additive number "951"
- **Neotame** (brand name: Newtame). This is a modified version of aspartame
- **Saccharin** (brand names: Sugar Twin, Sweet'N Low, Necta Sweet)
- **Sucralose** (brand name: Splenda).

There is a new artificial sweetener that does not have a brand name for the market place yet. It is called **advantame** and is a derivative of aspartame.

Artificial sweeteners are found in a variety of food and beverages labelled *"low sugar"*, *"diet"* or *"sugar-free"*, including soft drinks, chewing gum, candy, baked goods, fruit juice, ice cream and yogurt. So, make sure you are extra careful this week and check the food/beverage labels thoroughly for those often hidden artificial sweeteners.

Alternatives to sugar and artificial sweeteners

The alternatives to sugar and artificial sweeteners are less likely to cause a spike in blood sugar levels as they are absorbed more slowly by the body and are therefore a great choice for anxiety sufferers.

Here they are:

- **Xylitol**
  Xylitol is a naturally occurring alcohol found in low concentrations in many fruit and vegetable fibres. Commercially, it is extracted from corncobs and trees. Pure xylitol is a white crystalline substance that looks and tastes like sugar. It also contains roughly the same amount of sweetness as regular sugar. Unlike sugar or other sugar substitutes, it is actually beneficial for dental health. It is known for reducing cavities and re-mineralising damaged tooth enamel. Food labels may list the specific name, such as xylitol, or use the general term "sugar alcohol".

- **Honey**
  Honey is the least processed of the natural sweeteners as it is made by bees using nectar from flowers. It is made up of glucose, fructose and minerals such as iron, calcium, phosphate, sodium chloride, potassium and magnesium. It also has antioxidant, anti-bacterial, anti-fungal, anti-cancer and anti-inflammatory properties.

- **Maple syrup**
  Maple syrup is a natural sweetener that is made from the sap of the maple tree. The maple syrup itself is the sap that has been boiled until much of the water has evaporated leaving a thick, syrupy consistence. It has a caramel-like flavour and is twice as sweet as regular sugar. Make sure you are getting pure maple syrup and not maple-flavoured syrup which is usually a less expensive syrup (such as corn syrup) with a small amount of pure maple syrup or artificial maple extract.

- **Molasses**
  Molasses is made from sugarcane or sugar beets. It is a viscous by-product of the sugar refining process. It is quite thick (syrupy) and has a hearty, almost smoky taste. It is also sweeter than regular sugar. Molasses is commonly used in cooking, especially in cakes, cookies and other desserts. There are different kinds of molasses: light molasses, dark molasses and blackstrap molasses. Light molasses is the by-product from the first boiling cycle of sugarcane and contains the highest sugar

content. Dark molasses is the by-product of the second boiling cycle of sugarcane and contains less sugar than light molasses. Blackstrap molasses is the dark, bittersweet by-product of the third boiling cycle of sugarcane and contains the least sugar and the highest concentration of vitamins and minerals. Blackstrap molasses is also used as a remedy for anxiety.

Even these natural sweeteners shouldn't be consumed excessively as most of them do contain calories which can contribute to weight gain. Furthermore, Xylitol, for example, can cause temporary gastrointestinal side effects, such as bloating, flatulence and diarrhoea, due to its laxative effect when consumed in excess.

If you are a diabetic, consult your doctor or diet professional before incorporating any of these natural sugar substitutes into your diet.

Task 4: Practice: Meditation

This week, we are going to substitute your Belly Breathing practice from Week 1 with a meditation practice.

Meditation and its benefits

Meditation has become very popular in the last few years and it is very likely that you have heard about or may have even practiced it.

Meditation is the antidote to our fast-paced, high-demanding lives and is simply an exercise which helps to calm the mind and relax the body.

Meditation is beneficial for your emotional well-being as well as your overall health. It reduces stress and anxiety, relieves muscle tension, improves concentration, memory, emotional balance and sleep, generates optimism, self-esteem and more life satisfaction, increases immunity, lowers blood pressure, reduces inflammation in the body and restores a balanced function to the digestive system.

In meditation, your brain slows down from its normal, beta-wave activity to a calmer alpha state. This causes a sense of deep relaxation and peacefulness. However it is different to the relaxation gained from sleeping, as you stay alert and awake during meditation.

Meditation not only changes your immediate state of mind, but can also alter the structure of your brain, making you less susceptible to anxious feelings in the future.

There are many different types of meditation but they all have one thing in common – to focus on something, such as a visual object, a mantra or your breath. Focussing on one particular thing helps to anchor your thoughts and this quietens the mind. It also teaches you to be in the present moment rather than focusing on the past or the future. This is very helpful for anxiety sufferers as worrying and anxiety-producing thoughts are usually associated with the past or the future. Meditation can also help to identify thought patterns that contribute to anxiety. They may come up during meditation and this can be extremely helpful when trying to get to the bottom of your anxiety.

Meditation instruction

This meditation is a breath awareness meditation practice in which you are asked to focus on your breath. I personally think it is one of the easiest forms of meditation and it's great for beginners.

After this meditation practice, you are most likely to experience a sense of calmness as well as mental clarity.

As with the Belly Breathing practice from Week 1, make sure you are in a quiet place where you won't be disturbed for the next 10 minutes.

1. Lie on your back - either on a rug, blanket or yoga mat on the floor, or even in bed - with your knees bent and your feet on the floor/bed. Note: You can also do this practice in a seated position – on a chair, or in a cross-legged or kneeling position on the floor. The aim of the meditation practice is to stay awake and alert and therefore a lying position may not be suitable for everyone as it can cause you to fall asleep during the meditation. I suggest you try a few of the mentioned positions and see what works best for you.

2. If you are lying down, have your arms relaxed by your sides with the palms of your hands facing upwards. If you are in a seated position, place your hands loosely on your lap – the right hand on top of the left one with your palms facing upwards and the tips of your thumbs lightly touching.

3. Close your eyes.

4. Breathe in and out slowly through your nose if you can and if that feels comfortable for you. You can also breathe in through your nose and out through your mouth.

5. Now, take your awareness to your breath. It is easiest to focus on your breath by feeling how the breath moves in and out of your nostrils or by concentrating on the rising and falling of your chest or belly as you breathe in and out.

6. Continue for about 10 minutes. Make sure that you are not forcing your breath. Relax and breathe with ease. If your mind starts to wander and different thoughts are arising – which is very common – notice and acknowledge those thoughts and then gently bring your awareness back to your breath.

Once you are finished with your meditation in a lying position, roll onto your right side and stay there for a minute or two. Then slowly push yourself up to sitting and then standing. In a seated position, give yourself some time before getting up. By doing this, we want to make sure that we are cultivating the calmness we have gained through this practice.

If you happened to fall asleep during your meditation, don't feel bad about it. You gave your body what it needed most at the time, which was rest. And that is totally ok! Next time, maybe try a different meditation position or a different time.

Meditating can be a bit challenging to start with but the more you practice it, the better you will get and the more you will enjoy the benefits. Consistency in practice is the key and therefore it is best to meditate on a daily basis and preferably at similar times.

If you suffer from mild anxiety/stress, I suggest that you practice 10 minutes of Meditation each day.

If you suffer from moderate anxiety/stress, practice Meditation twice daily for 10 minutes (for example: 10 minutes in the morning and 10 minutes in the evening).

Summary of Week 2

- Eat foods that are rich in omega-3 fatty acids: oily fish (salmon, sardines, tuna, mackerel, trout), chia seeds, walnuts, Spirulina, flaxseed/linseed and its oil, olive oil
- Reduce sugar: cut down on white sugar; use sugar alternatives instead (xylitol, honey, maple syrup, molasses)
- Avoid artificial sweeteners: avoid *"low sugar"*, *"diet"* and *"sugar-free"* products
- Practice 10 minutes of Meditation daily

Action: Check out the meal plan as well as the recipes for Week 2 at the back of this book and start planning your week ahead.

This week's meal plan is intended to give you some suggestions and ideas on how to incorporate omega-3 rich foods into your diet while also maintaining a magnesium-rich diet at the same time.

Action: List all of your actions/ goals for Week 2.

For example:

To increase my omega-3 fatty acid intake I will eat …
To cut down on sugar I will not use any in my tea and avoid sugary foods (cakes, candy and soft drinks).
To avoid artificial sweeteners I will not buy any "diet" or "sugar-free" products.
I will do 10 minutes of Meditation at … each day.

My Action Plan – Week 2

✓	
✓	
✓	
✓	
✓	
✓	
✓	
✓	
✓	
✓	

Action: Practice some Meditation right now before reading on!

WEEK 3

We have almost reached the half-way point of this program! You are now well and truly in the middle of your journey to a calmer YOU. Take a couple of minutes to check in with your body and see how you are feeling. Are you noticing any improvements?

Ok, let's get into Week 3 of this program.

Your tasks for this week are:

- Apply dietary changes from Week 1 and 2
- Add foods that are high in tryptophan
- Avoid processed foods containing artificial colours, flavours and preservatives
- Practice 5-10 minutes of Alternate Nostril Breathing each day

Task 1: Applying dietary changes from Week 1 and 2

The first task of this week is to keep following the dietary changes from Week 1 and 2.

Avoid	Reduce	Keep eating
• Caffeine • Alcohol • Artificial sweeteners	• Sugar	• Magnesium-rich foods • Omega-3-fatty acid foods

Task 2: Adding foods that are high in Tryptophan

Anxiety Reliever: Tryptophan

Tryptophan is an essential amino acid which means it is essential for human life but it cannot be produced by the body and therefore must be part of our diet.

The body uses tryptophan for the production of the neurotransmitter serotonin which is known to improve mood and positive feelings. To be precise, tryptophan reacts with vitamins B6 and B3 in the presence of magnesium to produce serotonin. Serotonin is also the precursor to melatonin which has calming properties and promotes a restful sleep. High serotonin levels typically diminish anxiety.

Unsurprisingly, many anxiety sufferers tend to suffer from low serotonin levels. Improving serotonin levels by eating tryptophan-rich foods may have a significant impact on your journey to overcome anxiety.

Tip: Eating tryptophan-rich foods is not the only way you can increase the serotonin levels in your body. Serotonin is produced when bright light enters your eyes as well as when you exercise. So, make sure you also enjoy some outdoor activities on a regular basis. For example, go for a 20-30 minute walk each day.

Tryptophan-rich foods

All animal meat contains high levels of tryptophan but turkey has the highest. Because of the high tryptophan level, turkey will make you quite sleepy and is therefore great to eat at dinner time.

The following foods are high in tryptophan:

- Milk, yogurt, cheese
- Lentils
- Split peas
- Chicken
- Turkey.

Bananas (Week 1) and raw cacao products (Week 1) also contain tryptophan, so keep adding them to your diet as well.

Aim to include at least one tryptophan-rich food into your daily diet.

Task 3: Avoiding processed foods containing artificial colours, flavours and preservatives

Anxiety Stimulant: Processed foods containing artificial colours, flavours and preservatives

As we learnt in Week 2, processed foods are best to be avoided because most of them contain large amounts of added sugars. This week you will learn a few more reasons why they should be avoided or minimised.

Most processed foods contain artificial additives such as artificial colours and flavours as well as preservatives. Those food additives can aggravate your anxiety, especially if you are sensitive to them. They contain chemicals that have an effect on the neurotransmitters in your brain, causing nervous reactions. Therefore it is best to avoid them as much as you can.

Again, you need to take a close look at the ingredients list of the products you intend to purchase to check that they don't contain artificial colours, artificial flavours and preservatives.

Artificial colours

Artificial colours are used in many processed foods as they make the food more visually appealing to the consumer.

In the United States, the following seven artificial colourings are commonly used:

- **FD&C Blue No. 1 – Brilliant Blue FCF, E133 (blue shade)**
- **FD&C Blue No. 2 – Indigotine, E132 (indigo shade)**
- **FD&C Green No. 3 – Fast Green FCF, E143 (turquoise shade)**
- **FD&C Red No. 3 – Erythrosine, E127 (pink shade)**
- **FD&C Red No. 40 – Allura Red AC, E129 (red shade)**
- **FD&C Yellow No. 5 – Tartrazine, E102 (yellow shade)**
- **FD&C Yellow No. 6 – Sunset Yellow FCF, E110 (orange shade)**

Some of the food colourings have the abbreviation "FCF" in their names which stands for "For Colouring Food".

In Europe, "E" numbers 102-143 are used for artificial food colours. The most commonly used ones are:

- **E104: Quinoline Yellow**
- **E122: Carmoisine**
- **E124: Ponceau 4R**
- **E131: Patent Blue V**
- **E142: Green S**

Artificial Flavours

Artificial flavours are added to many processed foods to enhance their taste because over-processing (e.g. cooking, canning, freezing, dehydrating) destroys flavour.

They are made from chemicals instead of natural sources such as spices, fruits, fruit juice, vegetables, vegetable juice, herbs, plant material, meat, fish, poultry, eggs, dairy and fermentation products.

Chemically, the compounds used to produce artificial flavours are almost identical to those that occur naturally. The problem is not how the flavour additive is made, but it is the size of the dose consumed. Man-made flavours are very cheap and therefore are added in larger quantities than you would find in natural, unprocessed foods. Large doses of the chemicals contained in artificial flavours have been linked to a variety of health problems including anxiety.

Artificial flavours are usually listed as **"flavours"**, **"flavouring"**, **"artificial flavours"** or **"nature identical flavours"** in the ingredients.

Preservatives

Preservatives are used to give food a longer shelf life.

They can be identified by the numbers **200-290** or **E200-E290** on the ingredients list.

Here is a detailed list of commonly used preservatives:

E number	Chemical compound	Commonly used in:
200 or E200	Sorbic acid	Wine, cheese, other fermented products, dessert sauces and fillings, soups, sweets, drinks, yeast goods
201 or E201	Sodium sorbate	Wine, cheese, other fermented products, dessert sauces and fillings, soups, sweets
202 or E202	Potassium sorbate	Cheese, butter, yogurt, preserves, pickles, dried fruit, cakes, wine
203 or E203	Calcium sorbate	Fermented dairy produce, wine
210 or E210	Benzoic acid	Alcoholic beverages, baked goods, cheeses, gum, condiments, frozen dairy, relishes, soft sweets, cordials and sugar substitutes
211 or E211	Sodium benzoate	Orange diet soft drinks, milk and meat products, relishes and condiments, baked goods and lollies, maple syrup and margarine
212 or E212	Potassium benzoate	Margarine, pickles, fruit juice
213 or E213	Calcium benzoate	Fruit juice

E number	Chemical compound	Commonly used in:
214 or E214	Ethyl para-hydroxybenzoate	Beer, fruit preserves and juices, sauces, flavouring syrups, fruit desserts, processed fish
216 or E216	Propylparaben, Propyl para-hydroxybenzoate	Beer, fruit sauces, pickles and preserves, fruit desserts, fruit squashes and juices, processed fish
218 or E218	Methylparaben, Methyl para-hydroxybenzoate	Beer, fruit products, pickles, sauces, desserts, soft drinks, processed fish
220 or E220	Sulphur dioxide	Beer, soft drinks, dried fruit, juices, cordials, wine, vinegar, potato products
221 or E221	Sodium sulphite	Fresh fruit and vegetables, beer, wine, fruit juices and sauces, frozen shellfish
222 or E222	Sodium bisulphite, Sodium hydrogen sulphite	Beer, wine, cider, fruit squashes and juice, fresh fruit and vegetables, frozen shellfish, jams, pickles
223 or E223	Sodium metabisulphite	Preserved fruit and vegetables, pickles, fruit juice, frozen vegetables, frozen shellfish, dried fruits, fruit desserts
224 or E224	Potassium metabisulphite	Wine, frozen vegetables, fruit juice, fruit preserves, pickles, frozen shellfish
225 or E225	Potassium sulphite	Beer, soft drinks, dried fruit, juices, cordials, wine, vinegar, potato products
226 or E226	Calcium sulphite	Wine, fruit juice, canned fruit and vegetables, fruit pickles and preserves

E number	Chemical compound	Commonly used in:
227 or E227	Calcium hydrogen sulphite	Beer, canned fruit and vegetables, jams, pickles, fruit juice, fruit jelly
228 or E228	Potassium bisulphite, Potassium hydrogen sulphite	Beer, canned fruit and vegetables, jams, pickles, fruit juice, fruit jelly
233 or E233	Thiabendazole	Meat, milk
234 or E234	Nisin	Beer, processed cheese products, tomato paste
235 or E235	Natamycin, Pimaracin	Meat, cheese
239 or E239	Hexamethylene tetramine, Hexamine	Marinated fish
242 or E242	Dimethyl dicarbonate	Fruit drinks, sports drinks and wine
249 or E249	Potassium nitrite	Processed meats, cured and smoked meat and fish
250 or E250	Sodium nitrite	Processed meats, cured and smoked meat and fish
251 or E251	Sodium nitrate, Chile saltpetre	Processed meats, cured and smoked meat and fish
252 or E252	Potassium nitrate	Processed meats, cured and smoked meat and fish
260 or E260	Acetic acid	Fish fingers, butter, margarine, processed cheese, curry powder, cooking oil
261 or E261	Potassium acetate	Sauces, pickles

E number	Chemical compound	Commonly used in:
262 or E262	Sodium acetate, Sodium diacetate	Bouillons, bread, crisps and other snack foods, cheese, cakes
263 or E263	Calcium acetate	Packet desserts, pie fillings
270 or E270	Lactic acid	Sweets, dressings, soft drinks (sometimes beer), infant formulas and confectionary
280 or E280	Propionic acid	Bread cheese and flour products
281 or E281	Sodium propionate	Processed cheese and flour/bread products
282 or E282	Calcium propionate	Bakery products, dairy products
283 or E283	Potassium propionate	Bakery products, dairy products
290 or E290	Carbon dioxide	Wine, soft drinks, confectionary

I know this is a lot of information to digest and it will be a bit more time-consuming when you go food shopping this week. So here are some rules that may make it a little bit easier for you:

Rule No. 1: Processed foods are usually found in the centre aisles of your supermarket, so keep avoiding those as much as possible.

Rule No. 2: Choose foods with fewer and simpler ingredients.

Rule No. 3: Buy mostly fresh and whole foods.

Task 4: Practice: Alternate Nostril Breathing

Digging deeper into the breath

Continuing on from the topic "Breathing and Anxiety" from Week 1, I want to dive a bit deeper into this topic as it is very helpful for anxiety sufferers to understand the importance and power of the breath.

When our breathing is relaxed and we are healthy, our breathing alternates from one nostril to the other approximately every two hours. This natural right-left-nostril breathing rhythm creates a sense of calmness and balance in the body and mind.

Prolonged right-nostril breathing has a heating effect on the body, causing you to become more alert and active.

Prolonged left-nostril breathing, on the other hand, has a cooling effect on the body which will make you quieter and calmer, but also more passive and less alert.

Anxiety alters the natural right-left nostril breathing rhythm, causing prolonged right-nostril breathing.

The same way we were using the Belly Breathing exercise to restore a relaxing, diaphragmatic breath, there are breathing exercises that help restore the natural nostril alternation rhythm. The most commonly used breathing technique is called Nadi Shodhanam or Alternate Nostril Breathing. This breathing technique deliberately changes the flow of air from one nostril to the other by alternately closing off one nostril. This creates an even, regular rhythm which restores calmness and balance in body and mind.

Alternate Nostril Breathing instructions

Make sure you are in a quiet place where you won't be disturbed for the next 5-10 minutes.

During this breathing exercise, remember to breathe slowly and gently and most importantly without strain or the feeling of running out of breath.

1. Find a comfortable seated position – either on a chair, or in a cross-legged or kneeling position on the floor. Make sure your head, neck and torso are relatively erect.
2. Place the thumb of your right hand onto your right nostril, closing the right nostril off.
3. Inhale through the left nostril. At the end of the inhalation, close off that nostril with either the index or ring finger of your right hand and exhale through your right nostril. At the end of that exhalation, inhale through the same nostril (right nostril). Then, close off the right nostril with your thumb and exhale through the left nostril.
4. Continue with inhaling through your left nostril and complete step 3 two more times.
5. Take three breaths through both nostrils.
6. Repeat step 3 three times.
7. Take three breaths through both nostrils.
8. Repeat step 3 three times.

When you are finished with this breathing exercise, allo
or two before getting up.

If you suffer from mild anxiety/stress, practice Altern
once a day.

If you suffer from moderate anxiety/stress, practice Alternа.
Breathing twice a day.

...ary of Week 3

- Eat foods that are high in tryptophan: milk, yogurt, cheese, lentils, split peas, chicken, turkey
- Avoid processed foods containing artificial colours, flavours and preservatives: buy foods with fewer and simper ingredients; buy mostly fresh and whole foods
- Practice 5-10 minutes of Alternate Nostril Breathing daily

Action: Check out the meal plan as well as the recipes for Week 3 at the back of this book and start planning your week ahead.

This week's meal plan is intended to give you some suggestions and ideas on how to incorporate tryptophan-rich foods into your diet while also maintaining a magnesium and omega-3 rich diet at the same time.

Action: List all of your actions/ goals for Week 3.

For example:

To increase my tryptophan intake I will eat …
I will not buy any canned food or frozen dinners this week.
I will do 10 minutes of Alternate Nostril Breathing at … each day.

My Action Plan – Week 3

✓	
✓	
✓	
✓	
✓	
✓	
✓	
✓	
✓	
✓	

Action: Practice some Alternate Nostril Breathing right now before reading on!

WEEK 4

Week 4 – wow, this time is flying! Be proud of your achievements so far! I hope you are already feeling the amazing benefits of this program. Are you experiencing more calmness and an improvement in your overall wellbeing? Great, let's continue then.

This week, there will be more focus on anxiety-relieving practices. In addition to your daily breathing/meditation practice, we will incorporate a short yoga practice into your day which has been specifically designed to reduce anxiety.

Week 4's tasks are:

- Apply dietary changes from Week 1, 2 and 3
- Add foods that are rich in vitamin B
- Avoid refined grains
- Practice 10 minutes of Belly Breathing, Meditation or Alternate Nostril Breathing each day
- Practice Yoga for Anxiety 2-3 times during the week

Task 1: Applying dietary changes from Week 1, 2 and 3

The first task for Week 4 is to keep following the dietary changes from Week 1, 2 and 3.

Avoid	Reduce	Keep eating
• Caffeine • Alcohol • Artificial sweeteners • Processed foods containing artificial colours, flavours and preservatives	• Sugar	• Magnesium-rich foods • Omega-3-fatty acid foods • Tryptophan-rich foods

Task 2: Adding foods containing B vitamins

Anxiety Reliever: B vitamins

B vitamins are often called "anti-stress vitamins" but they not only relieve stress, they also reduce anxiety and depression. They play a role in several important processes in the body including the metabolism of carbohydrates, fats and proteins as well as the functioning of the immune system and nervous system.

Often referred to as vitamin B complex, these are the eight B vitamins:

- Thiamin (B1)
- Riboflavin (B2)
- Niacin (B3)
- Pantothenic Acid (B5)
- Pyridoxine (B6)
- Biotin (B7)
- Folic Acid or Folate (B9)
- Cobalamin (B12).

B vitamins are essential for the proper functioning of the nervous system. Deficiencies can lead to anxiety, irritability, fatigue and depression.

B vitamins have been found to stabilise the body's lactic acid levels. As panic disorder sufferers tend to generate excess lactic acid in their brains, B vitamins can be very helpful.

Several B vitamins, particularly vitamin B3, B6, B9 and B12, are directly or indirectly involved in the production of serotonin and other neurotransmitters. As we know, serotonin helps to regulate mood and relieves the symptoms of anxiety and depression.

Vitamin B1 is important for blood sugar control. As fluctuating blood sugars, in particular spikes and drops, can contribute to anxiety, this vitamin has a major impact on reducing anxiety and calming the nerves.

Vitamin B5 is essential for the adrenal glands and helps with managing stress and anxiety.

Though only some individual B vitamins have been highlighted here they are all equally important, especially for anxiety sufferers, and work best in synergy.

During times of stress, your body's demand for B vitamins increases. They are often depleted first. Also, during infection and when medications such as antibiotics, contraceptive pills and sleeping pills are taken, the need for B vitamins increases.

Vegetarians, in particular, are susceptible to B12 deficiencies because B12 is mostly found in animal products.

B vitamins are water-soluble and are not stored in the body and therefore must be included in the daily diet. They are very delicate and are easily destroyed, especially by alcohol and cooking. The western diet tends to be deficient in B vitamins because these vitamins are often removed during food processing. Refined grains, for example, lose a big proportion of B vitamins in the refining process. Therefore one of the tasks for this week is also to avoid refined grains and replace them with better vitamin B-rich choices.

B vitamin-rich foods

This week try to include at least two of the following vitamin B-rich foods into your diet each day:

- Brown rice
- Legumes (beans, peas and lentils)
- Wholegrain bread
- Mushrooms
- Avocado
- Wholegrain cereals
- Oats
- Eggs
- Beef
- Pork

- Chicken
- Fish
- Shellfish
- Milk and milk products.

You are already familiar with some of the vitamin B-rich foods listed here as they have also been listed as tryptophan-rich foods last week.

Task 3: Avoiding refined grains

Anxiety Stimulant: Refined grains

Refined grain foods include white bread, white rice, regular white pasta as well as other foods made with white flour (also called enriched wheat flour or all-purpose flour) such as cookies, cakes, pies, breakfast cereals and crackers.

Why are they so bad for anxiety sufferers?

Refined grains are quickly digested into simple sugars and are then rapidly absorbed into your bloodstream, almost as rapidly as refined sugars. This causes your blood sugar levels to spike and then quickly crash, contributing to anxiety.

Also, the refining process for grains strips away important vitamins. More than half of the B vitamins in wheat and 90 percent of vitamin E are lost in this process. As we have learnt, B vitamins help to ease stress and treat anxiety and depression.

Furthermore, refined grains cause inflammation in the body (the same as refined sugars) which can lead to anxiety as well as other modern day diseases such as depression, heart disease, obesity and cancer.

I believe those are all good reasons to avoid refined grains in our diet and replace them with healthier alternatives.

A great alternative to refined grains are whole grains which include:

- Whole wheat (e.g. Farro and kamut)
- Whole rye
- Barley (hulled and dehulled but not pearl)
- Buckwheat
- Spelt
- Quinoa
- Triticale
- Maize

- Millet
- Teff
- Amaranth
- Brown rice
- Wild rice
- Oats.

Refined grains products	Swap with	Whole grains products
White bread		• Whole wheat (also called wholegrain or wholemeal) bread • Wholegrain rye bread
Regular white pasta		• Whole wheat pasta • Spelt pasta • Brown rice pasta • Quinoa pasta • Soba (buckwheat) pasta
White rice		• Brown rice • Wild rice

Getting used to eating wholegrain products such as brown rice or whole wheat pasta may be a bit challenging to start with. If you don't immediately like the taste of brown rice, try adjusting your tastebuds slowly by mixing it with white rice and increasing the amounts of brown rice until you adapt. You can do the same with wholegrain pasta and white pasta.

Task 4: Practice: Breathing exercises or Meditation (from Week 1, 2 or 3)

This week you won't learn any new breathing or meditation technique. Instead it is up to you which of the breathing/meditation techniques from the previous three weeks you would like to practice. As you have become familiar with Belly Breathing, Alternate Nostril Breathing and Meditation previously, you may have noticed a preference for one of these techniques or one technique may work best for you. Practice that particular breathing or meditation exercise for 5-10 minutes each day. Or if you don't have a specific preference, you can alternate between the practices.

If you suffer from moderate anxiety, practice your preferred breathing/meditation technique twice daily.

On a day when you feel very anxious, practice more often or increase the time of your practice.

Task 5: Practice: Yoga for Anxiety

The following short yoga practice is great for calming your body and mind.

It can be done at any time during the day and even just before bedtime to promote a restful sleep. If you experience a lot of anxiety after waking up, this would be a great practice to do first thing in the morning. It will calm and ground you, and you will also feel refreshed at the same time.

The yoga poses in this practice are very gentle and suitable for beginners. However, if you do experience any pain or discomfort while doing one of those poses, gently ease out of the pose and rest for a while before continuing on with the practice. Leave out the pose that caused pain or discomfort.

These five yoga poses take about fifteen minutes. While they can be done daily, I suggest you practice at least 2 to 3 times per week for the remainder of this program.

PLEASE DO NOT EXERCISE IF:

You are feeling unwell, as it will be counter-productive.
You have eaten a heavy meal in the past two hours.
You have been drinking alcohol.
You have pain from an injury. Consult your doctor first; a rest may be needed before you exercise.
You have been taking painkillers as they may mask any warning signs of pain.
You are undergoing any medical treatment or taking any drugs. Please consult your doctor first.

PLEASE REMEMBER:

It is always advisable to consult your doctor before you begin any new exercise program and always stop if an exercise causes you pain.

Although some of these exercises may be fine for use during pregnancy I cannot recommend that you follow them, as I have not created this yoga practice with pregnancy in mind. Please check with your doctor.

Instructions:

These postures are best done on a soft surface, such as a rug, carpeted floor, blanket or large towel.

Make sure you wear comfortable clothing. Remove shoes and socks.

1. **Reclined Bound Angle Pose**

- Setup: Put a large pillow (or two sofa pillows) on the soft surface of your choice. Place a folded towel or blanket on the top end of your pillow as head support. Have two additional folded towels/blankets lying beside you – one on each side.
- Sit at the lower end of your pillow with your knees bent and feet placed on the floor (your buttocks stay on the floor) and then slowly roll your back onto the pillow. Rest your head on the folded towel/blanket placed on the top end of your pillow.

- Bring the soles of your feet together drawing them up gently toward your buttocks. Let your knees fall wide out to each side. Don't push or force your knees wide. Have them only as wide as feels comfortable for you and place a folded towel/blanket under each thigh as support.
- Have your arms wide, palms facing upwards.
- Close your eyes and relax.
- Stay in this pose for a few minutes (about 3-5 minutes or more if you like).
- To come out of this pose, bring your knees up and the soles of your feet onto the floor. Then roll onto your right side and push your upper body up to a seated position.
- Remove the pillow and towels/blankets as they are not needed for the rest of the exercises. You only need a soft surface to lie on.

2. Bridge Pose

Do not do this if you have or suffer from the following contraindication: neck injury, lower back injury, glaucoma, detached retina, high blood pressure (please check with your doctor if it is okay to do inverted yoga poses where the head is below the heart.)

Women specific contraindication: Avoid this pose during your period, especially in the first two days.

Bridge Pose 1

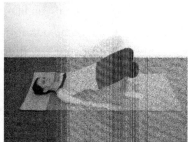
Bridge Pose 2

Bridge Pose 3

Bridge Pose 4

- Lie down on a soft surface/floor with your knees bent and feet placed hip-width apart on the mat. Bring your feet close to the buttocks, so that your heels are positioned under your knees. Your arms are beside your body with your palms facing down (see photo *Bridge Pose 1*).

- On the next exhale, lift your pelvis up off the floor – as high as it feels comfortable for you. Make sure that you don't strain your neck. Rest on your shoulder blades (see photo *Bridge Pose 2*).

- Inhale, bring your arms up toward the sky (see photo *Bridge Pose 3*).
- Exhale, move your arms over your head, resting them on the floor (see photo *Bridge Pose 4*).
- On the next inhale, bring your arms up toward the sky again and exhale them down to the floor beside your body.
- Inhale, and on the next exhale slowly release your back down to the floor – starting with the upper back, then the middle and lower back – basically rolling your spine down onto the floor, vertebrae by vertebrae.
- Repeat 4 more times.

3. Supine Twist

Do not do this if you have or suffer from the following contraindication: sacroiliac joint (SI joint) injury, herniated disk

Supine Twist 1

Supine Twist 2

Supine Twist 3

Supine Twist 4

- Lying on your back with your knees bent, hold your right knee with both hands and bring it towards your belly (see photo *Supine Twist 1*). Then, slowly straighten the left leg to rest on the floor (see photo *Supine Twist 2*).
- Now, hold the right knee with your left hand only. Your right arm extends out to the side, palm facing up (see photo *Supine Twist 3*). With the shoulders staying easy on the floor, slowly take your bent right leg across your body, so that your right hip lifts off the floor, twisting your lower torso (see photo *Supine Twist 4*). If your right shoulder and shoulder blade lift up off the floor, move your leg back to a point where your shoulders are easily on the floor.
- Take 5 slow and deep breaths while in this pose and then come back to the centre and switch sides.

- After you have done both sides, hug both knees into your chest. Stay in this pose for 2 full breaths and then slowly roll onto your right side and come up to standing.

4. Forward Bend (standing or seated)

You can do the forward bend either standing or seated on a chair. If you suffer from low blood pressure, do the version seated on a chair as forward bends can cause dizziness for people with low blood pressure.

Do not do this if you have or suffer from the following contraindication: disc problems, glaucoma, detached retina, high blood pressure (please check with your doctor if it is okay to do inverted yoga poses where the head is below the heart.)

Standing:

- Stand upright with your feet hip-width apart and your feet parallel. Your knees are slightly bent. Place your fingers on your hip creases - that's where your hip folds when you lift your leg.
- On the next exhale, bend forward at your hip creases (where your fingers are). Let your belly rest on your upper thighs. You may need to bend your knees more in order to do so.

Release your arms towards the floor. Your head and arms hang loosely and hands are resting on the floor (if they can comfortable reach that far). You can also hold your ankles or legs with your hands.

- Stay in this pose for up to ten breaths.
- To come out of this pose, on exhalation, slowly bring your upper body back up, rolling your spine up vertebrae by vertebrae, with your head coming up last.
- Allow yourself a few seconds to adjust to standing upright again. Most people will feel a little dizzy for about 20 seconds after coming up which is completely normal.

Note: You can also do this pose standing by a wall for support. Move about 8 to 12 inches (20 to 30 cm) away from the wall. Now, press your buttocks against the wall. Bend your knees and fold your upper body forward on exhalation, letting your head and arms hang loosely toward the floor. Your belly is resting on your upper thighs. Stay in this pose for up to ten breaths. To come out of this pose, follow the instructions above.

Seated on a chair:

- Sit comfortably on your chair. Feet and knees are hip-width apart, with feet flat on the floor.
- On the next exhale, lean forward, resting your belly and chest on your lap. If your chest doesn't reach your lap, place a pillow between your lap and chest. Let your head and arms hang loosely with your hands resting on the floor (if they can comfortable reach that far).
- Stay in this pose for up to ten breaths.
- To come out of this pose, on exhalation, slowly bring your upper body back up, rolling your spine up vertebrae by vertebrae, with your head coming up last.
- Rest in your chair for a few seconds before continuing with the next exercise.

5. Legs Up the Wall

Do not do this if you have or suffer from the following contraindication: high blood pressure (please check with your doctor if it is okay to do inverted yoga poses where the head is below the heart.)

- Setup: If your floor is not carpeted, place a blanket or large towel with the short side touching the wall to give you some padding for comfort.
- Come into this pose by sitting close to the wall with your right side facing it.
- Then, roll onto your back and raise your legs up against the wall. Your buttocks don't have to touch the wall. Six to 12 inches (15-30 cm) away from the wall is fine.
- Place your hands gently on your belly or have your arms wide with your palms facing upwards.
- Close your eyes and breathe slowly and deeply. Relax.
- Stay in this pose for a few minutes (about 3-5 minutes or more if you like).
- To come out of this pose, bring your knees towards your chest. Then roll onto your right side and push yourself up.

If your feet begin to tingle, if they "fall asleep" or become cold, bend your knees and bring them toward your belly until those feelings disappear. Then, raise your legs back up the wall.

Summary of Week 4

- Eat foods that are rich in B vitamins: brown rice, legumes (beans, peas, lentils), wholegrain bread, mushrooms, avocado, wholegrain cereals, oats, eggs, beef, pork, chicken, fish, shellfish, milk and milk products
- Avoid refined grains: buy wholegrain products instead, such as wholegrain bread, whole wheat pasta, spelt pasta, brown rice or wild rice
- Practice 10 minutes of Belly Breathing, Meditation or Alternate Nostril Breathing daily
- Practice Yoga for Anxiety 2-3 times during the week

Action: Check out the meal plan as well as the recipes for Week 4 at the back of this book and start planning your week ahead.

This week's meal plan is intended to give you some suggestions and ideas on how to incorporate vitamin B-rich foods into your diet while also maintaining a magnesium-, omega-3 and tryptophan-rich diet at the same time.

Action: List all of your actions/ goals for Week 4.

For example:
To increase my vitamin B intake I will eat …
I will buy wholegrain bread instead of white bread.
I will do 10 minutes of Belly Breathing at … each day.
I will practice Yoga for Anxiety on Monday, Wednesday and Friday afternoon.

My Action Plan – Week 4

✓	
✓	
✓	
✓	
✓	
✓	
✓	
✓	
✓	
✓	

Action: Practice the Reclined Bound Angle Pose from the Yoga for Anxiety practice right now before reading on!

WEEK 5

Final week!!! This is the homestretch. What a journey it has been, and I am so grateful to be able to share it with you.

The main focus of this final week will be to reinforce and keep following the good lifestyle habits we have been practicing over the past 4 weeks. Only one more food group will be added this week.

This week's tasks are:

- Apply dietary changes from Week 1-4
- Add foods that are rich in vitamin C
- Avoid foods containing MSG
- Practice 10 minutes of Belly Breathing, Meditation or Alternate Nostril Breathing each day
- Practice Yoga for Anxiety 2-3 times per week

Task 1: Applying dietary changes from Week 1-4

The first task of this final week is to continue applying the dietary changes from Week 1-4.

Avoid	Reduce	Keep eating
• Caffeine • Alcohol • Artificial sweeteners • Processed foods containing artificial colours, flavours and preservatives • Refined grains	• Sugar	• Magnesium-rich foods • Omega-3-fatty acid foods • Tryptophan-rich foods • Vitamin B-rich foods

Task 2: Adding foods rich in vitamin C

Anxiety Reliever: Vitamin C

It is widely known that vitamin C prevents the common cold due to its immune boosting properties but it is also a great stress buster and can decrease anxiety symptoms. Vitamin C plays an important role in the proper functioning of brain chemistry and adrenal glands and has been proven to reduce both the physical and psychological effects of stress on people.

Vitamin C is required for the synthesis of serotonin. This neurotransmitter, as we have already explored, helps to reduce anxiety symptoms.

When you are in a stressful situation, vitamin C is utilised by the adrenal glands in the production of the stress hormone cortisol. When there is not enough vitamin C available, the adrenal glands basically "panic" and release even more cortisol which then also increases anxiety.

Vitamin C is essential for everyone but it is especially important for anxiety sufferers as deficiencies impair the ability to respond to stress and cause anxiety symptoms such as restlessness, irritability, shakiness, fatigue and emotional instability.

Stress depletes C vitamins rapidly the same way it does with B vitamins. This can then lead to symptoms of anxiety caused by a deficiency in those vitamins. Therefore it is very important to consume more vitamin C-rich foods during anxious and stressful times.

Since the immune system is weakened by stress and anxiety making you more susceptible to infections, it is very beneficial for stress and anxiety sufferers to boost the immune system by increasing their vitamin C intake.

Vitamin C-rich foods

The best sources of vitamin C are fruit and vegetables, especially citrus fruits and red and green bell peppers (capsicums). It is best to consume them fresh and uncooked as the vitamin C content may be reduced by prolonged storage and cooking. Consider steaming, stir-frying or baking your vegetables instead of boiling them. For example, steaming reduces vitamin C by only 15% while boiling reduces it by 25%. Or you can reduce the cooking time and temperature to cut down the vitamin C loss.

It is recommended to store your vitamin C foods at room temperature as vitamin C is very sensitive to temperature. About 25 percent of the vitamin C can be lost during the freezing-thawing process.

Vitamin C is water-soluble and cannot be produced or stored by the body. Therefore vitamin C-rich foods need to be consumed on a daily basis.

As the body can only absorb a limited amount of vitamin C at a time (the rest is excreted), it is advisable to eat vitamin C-rich foods in smaller quantities frequently throughout the day. For example, an orange mid-morning and a kiwifruit after lunch, etc.

Foods that are rich in vitamin C are:

- Berries (e.g. strawberries, raspberries, cranberries)
- Brussels sprouts → also rich in magnesium
- Cauliflower
- Citrus fruits (e.g. oranges, grapefruit)
- Dark leafy greens (e.g. kale, spinach, broccoli) → also rich in magnesium
- Kiwifruit (Chinese gooseberries)
- Papaya (pawpaw)
- Parsley
- Pineapple
- Potatoes → also contain B vitamins
- Red and green bell peppers (capsicums)

- Sweet potatoes → also contain B vitamins
- Tomatoes.

It is recommended to eat at least 2 serves of fruit and 5 serves of vegetables/legumes per day. This includes all fruits and vegetables – not just those on our vitamins C-rich list.

For this program, I suggest you eat at least 1 banana and 1 vitamin C-rich fruit each day as well as 1 serving of dark green leafy vegetables (e.g. kale, spinach, broccoli) and at least 1-2 servings of other vitamin C-rich vegetables (e.g. potatoes, sweet potatoes, red and green bell peppers, etc.). Make sure you get the remaining 2-3 serves of vegetables/legumes each day as well. Those don't necessarily need to be vitamin-C rich vegetables, and could be avocados, carrots, beans, peas, etc.

The following table illustrates serving sizes for fruit and vegetables/legumes:

1 serve of fruit equals to:	• 1 medium piece, e.g. orange, banana • 2 small pieces, e.g. kiwifruit, apricots • 1 cup diced pieces or canned fruit • ½ cup juice
1 serve of vegetables or legumes equals to:	• ½ cup cooked vegetables • ½ cup cooked dried beans, peas or lentils • 1 cup salad vegetables • 1 medium potato

Tip: Try juicing your vitamin C-rich fruits and vegetables. But make sure you dilute your freshly squeezed fruit juices with water to reduce their fruit-sugar content. This will help to avoid blood-sugar fluctuations.

Task 3: Avoiding foods containing MSG

Anxiety Stimulant: Foods containing MSG

MSG stands for Monosodium Glutamate and is a form of concentrated salt which is added to foods to enhance their flavour. It intensifies the meaty, savoury taste of food and is favoured by the Japanese who describe it as the "fifth taste".

MSG is also called an excitotoxin and this name already tells us that it cannot be good for us, especially us anxiety sufferers.

The essential component of MSG is glutamate which occurs naturally in tomatoes, potatoes, mushrooms and other vegetables and fruits. Glutamate is also produced by the body in moderate amounts and acts as an "excitation" neurotransmitter. However, when it is consumed above what the body naturally produces, it not only overstimulates our taste buds, tricking our brain that a food item tastes good, but also overstimulates and disrupts our nervous system. This causes and exacerbates many health conditions including anxiety as well as depression, fibromyalgia, headaches/migraines, vision problems, digestive distress, heart attacks, hypertension, hyperactivity, asthma, obesity, infertility, chronic pain, fatigue, etc.

By increasing the excitability of neurons, excitotoxins like MSG eventually cause brain cells to die off which can lead to the development of degenerative diseases like Parkinson's, Huntington's, amyotrophic lateral sclerosis (ALS) or motor neurone disease (MND) and Alzheimer's.

Some people are more sensitive to MSG than others. While some people may not notice or may not be aware of any **symptoms**, others experience one or more of the following typical MSG sensitivity symptoms after eating food containing MSG:

- Headaches/migraines
- Nausea
- Digestive discomfort
- Diarrhoea
- Dizziness

- Drowsiness
- Numbness
- Flushing
- Sweating
- Tingling
- Weakness
- Heart palpitations
- Difficulty breathing
- Panic attacks.

Looking at what MSG does to our bodies and how it can trigger anxiety, it is evident that it should be avoided as much as possible.

Avoiding MSG is more difficult than it might sound because food companies are legally allowed to hide MSG on food labels under ingredient names like "natural flavour" and "yeast extract". There are dozens of innocent-sounding ingredient names that are used to hide synthesised MSG which makes it extremely difficult for consumers to identify.

So, you need to not only look out for **MSG (monosodium glutamate)** on the ingredients list but also for the following MSG aliases:

MSG aliases	Specific MSG alias names	Comments
Autolyzed *anything*	Autolyzed plant protein Autolyzed yeast Autolyzed yeast extract	
Barley malt	Barley malt	Often contains MSG
Bouillon	Bouillon	Often contains MSG
Brewer's yeast	Brewer's yeast	Often contains MSG
Broth	Broth	Often contains MSG
Carrageenan	Carrageenan	Often contains MSG
Anything caseinate	Calcium caseinate Sodium caseinate	

MSG aliases	Specific MSG alias names	Comments
Citric acid	Citric acid	Often contains MSG
Anything enzyme modified		
Anything containing enzymes		
Anything fermented		Most fermented foods such as soy sauce contain high levels of MSG.
Flavours/ flavouring	Beef flavouring Chicken flavouring Pork flavouring	Often contain MSG
Gelatine	Gelatine	Contains a tiny amount of MSG
Glutamic acid	Glutamic acid	
Anything glutamate	Monopotassium glutamate Calcium glutamate Monoammonium glutamate Magnesium glutamate	
Hydrolyzed *anything*	Acid-hydrolyzed vegetable protein (or HVP) Autolyzed yeast Hydrolyzed corn protein Hydrolyzed casein Hydrolyzed collagen Hydrolyzed collagen protein Hydrolyzed corn Hydrolyzed corn cereal solids Hydrolyzed corn gluten Hydrolyzed corn gluten protein Hydrolyzed corn protein	

MSG aliases	Specific MSG alias names	Comments
	Hydrolyzed corn soy wheat gluten protein	
	Hydrolyzed corn/soy/wheat protein	
	Hydrolyzed cornstarch	
	Hydrolyzed gelatine	
	Hydrolyzed milk protein	
	Hydrolyzed oat flour	
	Hydrolyzed plant protein	
	Hydrolyzed protein	
	Hydrolyzed soy	
	Hydrolyzed soy protein	
	Hydrolyzed soy wheat gluten protein	
	Hydrolyzed soy/corn protein	
	Hydrolyzed soy/corn/wheat protein	
	Hydrolyzed soy/wheat gluten protein	
	Hydrolyzed soya protein	
	Hydrolyzed soybean protein	
	Hydrolyzed torula and brewer's yeast protein	
	Hydrolyzed vegetable protein	
	Hydrolyzed vegetable protein powder	
	Hydrolyzed wheat	
	Hydrolyzed wheat gluten	
	Hydrolyzed wheat gluten protein	
	Hydrolyzed wheat protein	
	Hydrolyzed whey and casein protein	
	Hydrolyzed whey peptides	
	Hydrolyzed whey protein	
	Hydrolyzed whey protein concentrate	

MSG aliases	Specific MSG alias names	Comments
	Hydrolyzed whey protein isolate	
	Hydrolyzed yeast	
	Hydrolyzed yeast extract	
	Hydrolyzed yeast protein	
	Partially hydrolyzed beef stock	
	Partially hydrolyzed casein	
	Partially hydrolyzed guar gum	
	Partially hydrolyzed soybean	
	Partially hydrolyzed soybean oil	
	Partially hydrolyzed whey protein	
Malted barley	Malted barley	Often contains MSG
Malt extract	Malt extract	Often contains MSG
Maltodextrin	Maltodextrin	Often contains MSG
Natural flavours/ natural flavouring	Natural beef flavouring Natural chicken flavouring Natural pork flavouring	Often contain MSG
Nutritional yeast	Nutritional yeast	
Oligodextrin	Oligodextrin	Often contains MSG
Pectin	Pectin	Often contains MSG
Anything containing protease		
Anything protein	Plant protein Plant protein extract Soy protein Soy protein concentrate Soy protein isolate Textured protein Vegetable protein extract	

MSG aliases	Specific MSG alias names	Comments
	Whey protein Whey protein concentrate Whey protein isolate	
Anything protein fortified		
Seasonings	Seasonings	Often contain MSG
Soy sauce	Soy sauce	
Soy sauce extract	Soy sauce extract	
Stock	Stock	Often contains MSG
Torula yeast	Torula yeast	
Anything ultra-pasteurised		Often contains MSG
Yeast extract	Yeast extract	
Yeast food	Yeast food	
Yeast nutrient	Yeast nutrient	

As you can see, this list is very long and may not even contain all of the MSG aliases that are out on the market.

To make it a little easier for you, **avoid/be careful with** the following foods at the grocery store:

- Highly processed, flavourful (salty) snack-food
  - Flavoured chips
  - Flavoured crackers
  - Flavoured nuts
- Broths
  - Chicken broth
  - Beef broth
  - Non-organic vegetable broth
  - Bouillon cubes (chicken or beef)

- Soups
    - Broth-based soups (chicken noodle, vegetable soups)
    - Cream of ... soups (mushroom, chicken, celery, etc.)
    - Instant soup mixes
- Convenience Foods
    - Ramen noodles
    - Frozen dinners/foods
    - Certain Chinese foods
    - Flavour mixes
    - Dips
    - Sauces
    - Salad dressings
- Meats
    - Sausages
    - Hot dogs
    - Barbecued meats
    - Smoked meats
    - Processed deli meats (e.g. ham, bacon, salami, pastrami)

Note: This list is not exhaustive but it will give you a good idea which foods are most likely to contain MSG.

Here are a few additional tips on how to avoid MSG:

1. Steer clear of highly-processed as well as fast foods as most of them contain MSG.
2. Many Asian restaurants use MSG, so avoid eating Chinese or other Asian food, unless you prepare it yourself or you know with absolute certainty that the restaurant doesn't use MSG. You can, of course, specifically request "no MSG" to be used in your meal.
3. Use natural spices, herbs and vegetables to season and increase flavour in your dishes (e.g. sea salt, pepper, fresh garlic, onions, chili peppers, basil, etc.).
4. Use fresh produce (organic where possible) as much as you can.

Interesting fact: Magnesium can reduce the effects of MSG. This is another good reason for keeping your magnesium levels up, as you may still ingest MSG without even realising it.

Task 4: Practice: Breathing exercises or Meditation (from W 1, 2 or 3)

Continue on with your breathing/meditation practice from last week. Practice Belly Breathing, Alternate Nostril Breathing or Meditation 5-10 minutes daily.

If you suffer from moderate anxiety, it is recommended to practice twice daily.

Anytime you feel very anxious, practice more often or increase the length of time you practice.

k 5: Practice: Yoga for Anxiety

ie practicing Yoga for Anxiety from Week 4, two to three times per

e you noticed any changes in your anxiety levels after last week's yoga
actice?

Do you feel more grounded and calm after each practice?

Make sure you practice gently. If you experience any pain or discomfort,
stop immediately and come out of the pose. Then, rest for a short while
before continuing on with the practice, leaving out the pose that caused
pain or discomfort.

Summary of Week 5

- Eat foods that are rich in vitamin C: berries (strawberries, raspberries, cranberries), Brussels sprouts, cauliflower, citrus fruits (oranges, grapefruit), dark leafy greens (kale, spinach, broccoli), kiwifruit, papaya, parsley, pineapple, potatoes, red and green bell peppers, sweet potatoes, tomatoes
- Avoid foods containing MSG: avoid flavoured snack-food (chips, crackers), frozen dinners, flavour mixes as well as store-bought soups (especially instant soup mixes), broths, dips, sauces, salad dressings and processed deli meats
- Practice 10 minutes of Belly Breathing, Meditation or Alternate Nostril Breathing daily
- Practice Yoga for Anxiety 2-3 times during the week

Action: Check out the meal plan as well as the recipes for Week 5 at the back of this book and start planning your week ahead.

This week's meal plan is intended to give you some suggestions and ideas on how to incorporate vitamin C-rich foods into your diet while also maintaining a magnesium, omega-3, tryptophan, and vitamin B-rich diet at the same time.

Action: List all of your actions/ goals for Week 5.

For example:
To increase my vitamin C intake I will eat …
I will not buy any flavoured potato chips, instant soup mixes or frozen dinners this week.
I will do 10 minutes of Meditation at … each day.
I will practice Yoga for Anxiety on Monday, Wednesday and Friday afternoon.

My Action Plan – Week 5

✓	
✓	
✓	
✓	
✓	
✓	
✓	
✓	
✓	
✓	

Action: Practice the Legs Up the Wall Pose from the Yoga for Anxiety practice right now before reading on!

WEEK 6 AND BEYOND

Congratulations!!! You have successfully completed the program "Calm Your Mind in 5 Weeks" and established healthy lifestyle changes to reduce or overcome your anxicty naturally. So keep doing what you are doing – that means keep repeating Week 5 of this program over and over again. This will help you to remain as calm and relaxed as you are right now and even show further improvements over the coming months and years.

As a little reminder:

Avoid	Reduce	Keep eating	Practice
Caffeine	Sugar	Magnesium-rich foods	**5-10 minutes** of Belly Breathing, Alternate Nostril Breathing or Meditation **daily**
Alcohol			
Artificial sweeteners		Omega-3-fatty acid foods	
		Tryptophan-rich foods	Yoga for Anxiety **2-3 times per week**
Processed foods containing artificial colours, flavours and preservatives		Vitamin B-rich foods	
		Vitamin C-rich foods	
Refined grains			
Foods containing MSG			

Cheers to a healthy, happy, calm and relaxed YOU!

All the best,

Jacqueline Brandes

PROGRAM TABLE

Week 1	Week 2	Week 3	Week 4	Week 5
	Apply dietary changes from Week 1	Apply dietary changes from Week 1 and 2	Apply dietary changes from Week 1, 2 and 3	Apply dietary changes from Week 1-4
Add foods that are high in **magnesium**	Add foods that are rich in **omega-3 fatty acids**	Add foods that are high in **tryptophan**	Add foods that are rich in **vitamin B**	Add foods that are rich in **vitamin C**
• Almonds • Avocados • Bananas • Dark chocolate/ raw cacao • Dark leafy greens (e.g. spinach, kale or broccoli) • Quinoa	• Oily fish (e.g. salmon, sardines, tuna, mackerel or trout) • Chia seeds • Walnuts • Spirulina • Flaxseed/ linseed and its oil • Olive oil	• Milk, yogurt, cheese • Lentils • Split peas • Chicken • Turkey	• Brown rice • Legumes (beans, peas and lentils) • Wholegrain bread • Mushrooms • Avocado • Wholegrain cereals • Oats • Eggs • Beef • Pork • Chicken • Fish • Shellfish • Milk and milk products	• Berries • Brussels sprouts • Cauliflower • Citrus fruits (e.g. oranges, grapefruit) • Dark leafy greens (e.g. spinach, broccoli) • Kiwifruit (Chinese gooseberries) • Papaya (pawpaw) • Parsley • Pineapple • Potatoes • Red and green bell peppers (capsicums) • Sweet potatoes • Tomatoes

Week 1	Week 2	Week 3	Week 4	Week 5
Avoid **caffeine** and **alcohol**	Reduce **sugar** and avoid all **artificial sweeteners**	Avoid **processed foods** containing **artificial colours, flavours and preservatives**	Avoid **refined grains**	Avoid foods containing **MSG**
Alternatives:	**Alternatives:**	**Tips:**	**Alternatives:**	**Avoid:**
• Herbal teas (e.g. Peppermint, Green, Chamomile, Lemon Balm/ Melissa, Lavender, Rooibos, Passionflower, Hawthorn tea) • Fruit teas • Decaffeinated coffee • Caffeine-free coffee (e.g. Spelt or Dandelion coffee) • Water	• Xylitol • Honey • Maple syrup • Molasses **Avoid:** • "low sugar", "diet" and "sugar-free" products	• Buy mostly fresh and whole foods • Choose foods with fewer and simpler ingredients • Avoid the centre aisles in the supermarket – shop the outside	• Whole wheat/ wholegrain/ wholemeal bread • Wholegrain rye bread • Whole wheat pasta • Spelt pasta • Brown rice pasta • Quinoa pasta • Soba (buckwheat) pasta • Brown rice • Wild rice	• Flavoured chips, crackers, nuts • Bouillon cubes • Instant soup mixes • Frozen dinners • Chinese/ Asian foods • Flavour mixes • Dips, sauces, salad dressings

Week 1	Week 2	Week 3	Week 4	Week 5
Practice: Belly Breathing	Practice: Meditation	Practice: Alternate Nostril Breathing	Practice: Breathing exercises or Meditation (from Week 1, 2 or 3)	Practice: Breathing exercises or Meditation (from Week 1, 2 or 3)
10 minutes daily	10 minutes daily	5-10 minutes daily	10 minutes daily	10 minutes daily
			Practice: Yoga for Anxiety	Practice: Yoga for Anxiety
			2-3 times per week	2-3 times per week

MEAL PLAN

Week 1

	Breakfast	Mid-morning Snack	Lunch	Mid-afternoon Snack	Dinner
Monday	Porridge (Oatmeal) with Banana, Cinnamon, Almonds & Coconut Milk	1 banana or Banana and Almond Smoothie	Open-Faced Avocado Sandwich	A handful of almonds/ some dark chocolate or 1 Bliss Ball* (Cacao and Almond Bliss Balls)	Pasta with Broccoli and Pine Nuts
Tuesday	Spinach and Poached Egg Toast	1 banana or Banana and Greens Smoothie	Ham, Cheese and Spinach Sandwich	A handful of almonds/ some dark chocolate or 1 Bliss Ball	Grilled Fish with Quinoa Salad
Wednesday	Banana Cacao Overnight Oats*	1 banana or Banana and Almond Smoothie	Quinoa Salad with Avocado and Tomatoes*	A handful of almonds/ some dark chocolate or 1 Bliss Ball	Steak with Roast Potatoes and Broccoli

	Breakfast	Mid-morning Snack	Lunch	Mid-afternoon Snack	Dinner
Thursday	Avocado and Poached Egg Toast	1 banana or Banana and Greens Smoothie	Chicken Avocado Sandwich	A handful of almonds/ some dark chocolate or 1 Bliss Ball	Spaghetti with Spinach and Garlic
Friday	Quinoa Porridge (Oatmeal) with Banana, Cinnamon and Almonds	1 banana or Banana and Almond Smoothie	Roast Beef, Cheese and Spinach Sandwich	A handful of almonds/ some dark chocolate or 1 Bliss Ball	Chicken and Broccoli Stir-Fry with Rice
Saturday	Banana Pancakes	1 banana or Banana and Greens Smoothie	Broccoli Soup	A handful of almonds/ some dark chocolate or 1 Bliss Ball	Pork with Sweet Potato Chips and Wilted Spinach
Sunday	Spinach and Mushroom Scrambled Eggs	1 banana or Banana and Almond Smoothie	Grilled Chicken Breast with Avocado and Spinach Salad	A handful of almonds/ some dark chocolate or 1 Bliss Ball	Ground Beef-Stuffed Capsicum (Bell Pepper) with Quinoa

* prepare the night before

Quick & easy ideas for breakfast:

- Add 1 sliced banana and/or some almonds (up to a handful, sliced or whole) to your usual muesli, cereal or porridge (oatmeal)

- Add some spinach to your scrambled eggs

Quick & easy ideas for lunch:

- Add some fresh spinach leaves to your sandwich or wrap

- Use avocado instead of butter for your sandwich

Quick & easy ideas for dinner:

- Add steamed broccoli as a side dish to your meal

- Add steamed spinach or kale as a side dish to your meal

- Add quinoa as a side dish to your usual steak/pork/chicken/fish and vegetables meal

- Prepare your favourite rice dish and use quinoa instead of rice

Week 2

	Breakfast	Mid-morning Snack	Lunch	Mid-afternoon Snack	Dinner
Monday	Porridge (Oatmeal) with Banana, Cinnamon, Almonds & Coconut Milk + Flaxseeds or Walnuts	1 banana or Banana and Almond Smoothie with Spirulina	Smoked Salmon Sandwich with Cream Cheese, Capers and Spinach	A handful of almonds or walnuts/ some dark chocolate or 1 Bliss Ball* (Cacao and Almond Bliss Balls)	Grilled Chicken with Mashed Potatoes and Broccoli
Tuesday	Spinach and Poached Egg Toast (with smoked salmon slices)	1 banana or Banana and Greens Smoothie with Spirulina	Open-Faced Avocado Sandwich	A handful of almonds or walnuts/ some dark chocolate or 1 Bliss Ball	Pasta with Broccoli and Pine Nuts
Wednesday	Banana Cacao Overnight Chia Pudding*	1 banana or Chocolate-Chia Smoothie	Cream Cheese, Black Olive, Walnut and Spinach Sandwich	A handful of almonds or walnuts/ some dark chocolate or 1 Bliss Ball	Quinoa Stir-Fry with Vegetables and Chicken

	Breakfast	Mid-morning Snack	Lunch	Mid-afternoon Snack	Dinner
Thursday	Quinoa Porridge (Oatmeal) with Banana, Cinnamon and Almonds + Flaxseeds or Walnuts	1 banana or Green Smoothie with Flaxseed	Ham Sandwich with Avocado Spread	A handful of almonds or walnuts/ some dark chocolate or 1 Bliss Ball	Spaghetti with Spinach and Garlic
Friday	Banana Cacao Overnight Oats with Chia Seeds*	1 banana or Banana and Almond Smoothie with Spirulina	Chicken Sandwich with Apple, Walnut and Spinach	A handful of almonds or walnuts/ some dark chocolate or 1 Bliss Ball	Grilled Fish with Quinoa Salad (use salmon fillets)
Saturday	Banana Pancakes with Flaxseeds	1 banana or Banana and Greens Smoothie with Spirulina	Tuna Quinoa Salad*	A handful of almonds or walnuts/ some dark chocolate or 1 Bliss Ball	Steak with Roast Potatoes and Broccoli
Sunday	Avocado and Poached Egg Toast (with smoked salmon slices)	1 banana or Chocolate-Chia Smoothie	Grilled Chicken Breast with Avocado, Spinach and Walnut Salad	A handful of almonds or walnuts/ some dark chocolate or 1 Bliss Ball	Pork with Sweet Potato Chips and Wilted Spinach

* prepare the night before

Quick & easy ideas for breakfast:

- Add 1 sliced banana and your choice of 1 tablespoon of ground flaxseeds, 1 tablespoon of chia seeds or some walnuts (up to a handful) to your usual muesli, cereal or porridge (oatmeal)

  Note: You can also add all three Omega-3-rich foods, the ground flaxseeds, chia seeds and walnuts, to your usual muesli, cereal or porridge (oatmeal).

  Tip: Add a sprinkle of cinnamon to combat sugar cravings.

Quick & easy ideas for lunch:

- Add smoked salmon or tuna to your sandwich

- Add a salad drizzled with olive oil, flaxseed oil or a mix of olive and flaxseed oil to your lunch

Quick & easy ideas for dinner:

- Use olive oil for cooking at low to medium temperatures

- Use olive oil or flaxseed oil or a mix of both for side salads

- Add steamed broccoli as a side dish and drizzle with some flaxseed oil

- Add mashed potatoes as a side dish and use flaxseed oil instead of butter and milk

- Prepare a pasta dish and drizzle some flaxseed oil over the pasta

- Prepare a fish dish using oily fish (salmon, tuna, mackerel or trout)

Week 3

	Breakfast	Mid-morning Snack	Lunch	Mid-afternoon Snack	Dinner
Monday	Banana Cacao Overnight Oats with Chia Seeds*	1 banana or Banana and Almond Smoothie with Spirulina	Open-Faced Avocado Sandwich with Feta Cheese	A handful of almonds or walnuts/ some dark chocolate or 1 Bliss Ball* (Cacao and Almond Bliss Balls)	Ground Turkey with Rice and Spinach
Tuesday	Porridge (Oatmeal) with Banana, Cinnamon, Almonds & Coconut Milk + Flaxseeds or Walnuts	1 banana or Banana and Greens Smoothie with Spirulina	Turkey Sandwich with Avocado, Brie Cheese, Cranberry Sauce and Spinach	A handful of almonds or walnuts/ some dark chocolate or 1 Bliss Ball	Quinoa Stir-Fry with Vegetables and Chicken
Wednesday	Avocado and Poached Egg Toast (with smoked salmon slices)	1 banana or Chocolate-Chia Smoothie	Smoked Salmon Sandwich with Cream Cheese, Capers and Spinach	A handful of almonds or walnuts/ some dark chocolate or 1 Bliss Ball	Pasta with Broccoli and Pine Nuts

	Breakfast	Mid-morning Snack	Lunch	Mid-afternoon Snack	Dinner
Thursday	Banana Cacao Overnight Chia Pudding*	1 banana or Green Smoothie with Flaxseed	Turkey Sandwich with Avocado, Spinach and Tomato	A handful of almonds or walnuts/ some dark chocolate or 1 Bliss Ball	Pan-Seared Salmon with Lentil and Quinoa Salad
Friday	Quinoa Porridge (Oatmeal) with Banana, Cinnamon and Almonds + Flaxseeds or Walnuts	1 banana or Banana and Almond Smoothie with Spirulina	Chicken Sandwich with Avocado, Brie Cheese and Spinach	A handful of almonds or walnuts/ some dark chocolate or 1 Bliss Ball	Pan-Seared Turkey Cutlets with Roast Potatoes and Broccoli
Saturday	Banana Pancakes with Flaxseeds	1 banana or Banana and Greens Smoothie with Spirulina	Grilled Chicken Breast with Spinach, Walnut and Feta Salad	A handful of almonds or walnuts/ some dark chocolate or 1 Bliss Ball	Spaghetti with Spinach and Garlic
Sunday	Spinach and Poached Egg Toast (with smoked salmon slices)	1 banana or Chocolate-Chia Smoothie	Warm Lentil, Quinoa and Spinach Salad	A handful of almonds or walnuts/ some dark chocolate or 1 Bliss Ball	Steak with Broccoli and Baked Potato with Sour Cream

* prepare the night before

Quick & easy ideas for breakfast:

- Add 1 sliced banana and your choice of 1 tablespoon of ground flaxseeds, 1 tablespoon of chia seeds or some walnuts or almonds (up to a handful) to your usual muesli, cereal or porridge (oatmeal)

- Use milk or yogurt with your muesli/cereal

Quick & easy ideas for lunch:

- Add smoked turkey to your sandwich (for example: smoked turkey sandwich with avocado)

- Add chicken (either grilled chicken or chicken deli meat) to your sandwich (for example: chicken sandwich with avocado)

- Add cheese to your sandwich

Quick & easy ideas for dinner:

- Prepare a turkey dish

- Prepare a chicken dish

- Prepare a lentil dish

- Prepare a split peas dish

- Prepare a dish using milk, yogurt or cheese

Week 4

	Breakfast	Mid-morning Snack	Lunch	Mid-afternoon Snack	Dinner
Monday	Quinoa Porridge (Oatmeal) with Banana, Cinnamon and Almonds + Flaxseeds or Walnuts	1 banana or Banana and Almond Smoothie with Spirulina	Turkey Sandwich with Avocado, Spinach and Tomato (on wholegrain or wholemeal bread)	A handful of almonds or walnuts/ some dark chocolate or 1 Bliss Ball* (Cacao and Almond Bliss Balls)	Pasta with Broccoli and Pine Nuts (use whole wheat or spelt pasta)
Tuesday	Spinach and Poached Egg Toast (with smoked salmon slices; use wholegrain or wholemeal bread)	1 banana or Banana and Greens Smoothie with Spirulina	Chicken Sandwich with Avocado, Brie Cheese and Spinach (on wholegrain or wholemeal bread)	A handful of almonds or walnuts/ some dark chocolate or 1 Bliss Ball	Pan-Seared Salmon with Lentil and Quinoa Salad

	Breakfast	Mid-morning Snack	Lunch	Mid-afternoon Snack	Dinner
Wednesday	Banana Cacao Overnight Oats with Chia Seeds*	1 banana or Chocolate-Chia Smoothie	Smoked Salmon Sandwich with Cream Cheese, Capers and Spinach (on wholegrain or wholemeal bread)	A handful of almonds or walnuts/ some dark chocolate or 1 Bliss Ball	Chicken and Broccoli Stir-Fry with Brown Rice
Thursday	Avocado and Poached Egg Toast (with smoked salmon slices; use wholegrain or wholemeal bread)	1 banana or Green Smoothie with Flaxseed	Open-Faced Avocado Sandwich with Feta Cheese (on wholegrain or wholemeal bread)	A handful of almonds or walnuts/ some dark chocolate or 1 Bliss Ball	Ground Turkey-Stuffed Capsicum (Bell Pepper) with Quinoa
Friday	Porridge (Oatmeal) with Banana, Cinnamon, Almonds & Coconut Milk + Flaxseeds or Walnuts	1 banana or Banana and Almond Smoothie with Spirulina	Turkey Sandwich with Avocado, Brie Cheese, Cranberry Sauce and Spinach (on wholegrain or wholemeal bread)	A handful of almonds or walnuts/ some dark chocolate or 1 Bliss Ball	Spaghetti with Spinach and Garlic (use whole wheat spaghetti; can also add some mushrooms)

	Breakfast	Mid-morning Snack	Lunch	Mid-afternoon Snack	Dinner
Saturday	Banana Pancakes with Flaxseeds	1 banana or Banana and Greens Smoothie with Spirulina	Grilled Chicken Breast with Spinach, Walnut and Feta Salad	A handful of almonds or walnuts/ some dark chocolate or 1 Bliss Ball	Ground Turkey with Brown Rice, Spinach and Mushrooms
Sunday	Spinach and Mushroom Scrambled Eggs	1 banana or Chocolate-Chia Smoothie	Warm Lentil, Quinoa and Spinach Salad	A handful of almonds or walnuts/ some dark chocolate or 1 Bliss Ball	Steak with Creamy Mushroom Sauce, Sweet Potato Chips and Broccoli

* prepare the night before

Quick & easy ideas for breakfast:

- Add 1 sliced banana and your choice of 1 tablespoon of ground flaxseeds, 1 tablespoon of chia seeds or some walnuts or almonds (up to a handful) to your usual muesli, cereal or porridge (oatmeal)

- Use milk or yogurt with your muesli/cereal

- Use eggs for breakfast (scrambled, poached, etc.)

- Use wholegrain or wholemeal bread for your toast

- Add mushrooms to your scrambled eggs

Quick & easy ideas for lunch:

- Use wholegrain or wholemeal bread or wraps

Quick & easy ideas for dinner:

- Use whole wheat pasta instead of normal pasta

- Add brown rice as a side dish to your usual steak/pork/chicken/fish and vegetables meal

- Add beans or peas as a side dish

Week 5

	Breakfast	Mid-morning Snack	Lunch	Mid-afternoon Snack	Dinner
Monday	Quinoa Porridge (Oatmeal) with Banana, Cinnamon and Almond + Flaxseeds or Walnuts (add berries or other chopped fruit)	1 banana or Banana and Almond Smoothie with Spirulina	Turkey Sandwich with Avocado, Spinach and Tomato	A handful of almonds or walnuts/ some dark chocolate or 1 Bliss Ball* (Cacao and Almond Bliss Balls)	Pasta with Broccoli and Pine Nuts (use whole wheat or spelt pasta)
Tuesday	Acai Bowl	1 banana or Banana and Greens Smoothie with Spirulina and Berries	Chicken Sandwich with Avocado, Brie Cheese and Spinach	A handful of almonds or walnuts/ some dark chocolate or 1 Bliss Ball	Ground Turkey-Stuffed Capsicum (Bell Pepper) with Quinoa

	Breakfast	Mid-morning Snack	Lunch	Mid-afternoon Snack	Dinner
Wednesday	Banana Cacao Overnight Oats with Chia Seeds* or Banana Cacao Overnight Chia Pudding* (add berries or other chopped fruit)	1 banana or Chocolate-Chia Smoothie	Smoked Salmon Sandwich with Cream Cheese, Capers and Spinach	A handful of almonds or walnuts/ some dark chocolate or 1 Bliss Ball	Grilled Chicken with Mashed Potatoes and Broccoli
Thursday	Avocado and Poached Egg Toast (with smoked salmon slices; add a fresh tomato on the side)	1 banana or Green Smoothie with Flaxseed and Berries	Open-Faced Avocado Sandwich with Feta Cheese (garnish with some tomato slices)	A handful of almonds or walnuts/ some dark chocolate or 1 Bliss Ball	Spaghetti with Spinach and Garlic (use whole wheat spaghetti; can also add some mushrooms)
Friday	Porridge (Oatmeal) with Banana, Cinnamon, Almonds & Coconut Milk + Flaxseeds or Walnuts (add berries or other chopped fruit)	1 banana or Banana and Almond Smoothie with Spirulina	Turkey Sandwich with Avocado, Brie Cheese, Cranberry Sauce and Spinach	A handful of almonds or walnuts/ some dark chocolate or 1 Bliss Ball	Pan-Seared Salmon with Lentil and Spinach Salad

	Breakfast	Mid-morning Snack	Lunch	Mid-afternoon Snack	Dinner
Saturday	Banana Pancakes with Flaxseeds (add berries)	1 banana or Banana and Greens Smoothie with Spirulina and Berries	Grilled Chicken Breast with Spinach, Walnut and Feta Salad	A handful of almonds or walnuts/ some dark chocolate or 1 Bliss Ball	Ground Turkey with Brown Rice, Spinach and Mushrooms
Sunday	Spinach and Mushroom Scrambled Eggs	1 banana or Chocolate-Chia Smoothie	Warm Lentil, Quinoa and Spinach Salad	A handful of almonds or walnuts/ some dark chocolate or 1 Bliss Ball	Steak with Creamy Mushroom Sauce, Sweet Potato Chips and Broccoli

* prepare the night before

Quick & easy ideas for breakfast:

- Add 1 sliced banana, 1-2 tablespoons of berries and your choice of 1 tablespoon of ground flaxseeds, 1 tablespoon of chia seeds or some walnuts or almonds (up to a handful) to your usual muesli, cereal or porridge (oatmeal)

- Yogurt with chopped fruit and/or berries

Quick & easy ideas for lunch:

- Add some tomato slices to your sandwich

- Garnish your sandwich with parsley

- Add a salad to your lunch

Quick & easy ideas for dinner:

- Add broccoli, cauliflower or Brussels sprouts as a side dish

- Add sweet potatoes or potatoes as a side dish

- Add a side salad to your meal

RECIPES

Breakfasts

Acai Bowl

Serves: 1

Ingredients

2 frozen Acai smoothie packs (for example: Amazonia or Sambazon
Acai Smoothie Packs, usually available at health food stores or
online)
1 banana, sliced and frozen*
⅓ cup coconut water or apple juice
Toppings: your choice of fresh blueberries or other berries/fruit, sliced
banana, shredded coconut, crumbled granola, etc.

Instructions

Blend the 2 frozen Acai packs, frozen banana and coconut water in
a blender until it is a thick and creamy smoothie-like consistency. Put
the mixture in a breakfast bowl and top with your choice of toppings.

* Freeze peeled and sliced ripe bananas for easier blending.

Avocado and Poached Egg Toast

Serves: 1

Ingredients

2 eggs
2 slices of bread (preferably wholegrain or wholemeal bread)
½ avocado, skin and seed removed
Salt and pepper, to taste

Instructions

Bring a saucepan of water to a rolling boil. Break one egg at a time and carefully slide it into the boiling water. Put a lid on the saucepan and turn off the heat. Leave the eggs to cook in the hot water for 3 minutes.

While the eggs are cooking, toast your 2 slices of bread. Spread the avocado evenly onto the toasted bread.

To serve, place one poached egg on top of each slice of bread and sprinkle with some salt and black pepper.

Banana Cacao Overnight Chia Pudding

Serves: 1

Ingredients

3 tbsps chia seeds
¾ cup coconut milk or almond milk (unsweetened)
1 banana, sliced
½ tbsp raw cacao powder (unsweetened)
Drizzle of honey or maple syrup

Instructions

Mix the chia seeds with the milk, cover and leave in the refrigerator overnight to soak. In the morning, take the chia mix out of the fridge and give it a quick stir. Mix in the cacao powder and banana slices and add a drizzle of honey or maple syrup.

Banana Cacao Overnight Oats – Week 1

Serves: 1

Ingredients

4 tbsps rolled oats, uncooked
6 tbsps milk (cow, almond, coconut milk, etc.)
4 tbsps Greek yogurt
1 tbsp raw cacao powder (unsweetened)
1 banana, sliced
A drizzle of honey, to taste

Instructions

Combine oats, milk, yogurt, cacao powder and honey in a breakfast bowl. Add banana slices and stir until mixed throughout. Cover and refrigerate overnight.

Banana Cacao Overnight Oats with Chia Seeds – Week 2-5

Serves: 1

Ingredients

- 4 tbsps rolled oats, uncooked
- 1 tbsp chia seeds
- 6 tbsps milk (cow, almond, coconut milk, etc.)
- 4 tbsps Greek yogurt
- 1 tbsp raw cacao powder (unsweetened)
- 1 banana, sliced
- A drizzle of honey, to taste

Instructions

Combine oats, chia seeds, milk, yogurt, cacao powder and honey in a breakfast bowl. Add banana slices and stir until mixed throughout. Cover and refrigerate overnight.

Banana Pancakes – Week 1

Serves: 1

Ingredients

6 tbsps self-raising flour (preferably wholemeal flour)
8 tbsps milk (add a little more milk if necessary)
1 egg
1 tsp olive oil (or coconut oil)
1 banana, thinly sliced
Honey or maple syrup, to taste
Optional spices to add to the batter: 1 tsp ground cinnamon or nutmeg

Instructions

Combine flour, milk and egg and whisk or blend until smooth. Let the batter sit for about 2-3 minutes.

Warm the oil in a non-stick frying pan over medium heat. Spoon ¼ cup batter into the pan and cook for 2 to 3 minutes or until bubbles appear on the surface. Turn the pancake over and cook the other side for 1 to 2 minutes or until golden and cooked through. Transfer the pancake to a plate and cover to keep warm. Repeat with the remaining batter to make 3 pancakes.

Top the pancakes with the sliced banana and some honey or maple syrup to taste.

Banana Pancakes with Flaxseeds – Week 2-5

Serves: 1

Ingredients

6 tbsps self-raising flour (preferably wholemeal flour)
1 tbsp ground flaxseeds
8 tbsps milk (add a little more milk if necessary)
1 egg
1 tsp olive oil (or coconut oil)
1 banana, thinly sliced
Honey or maple syrup, to taste
Optional spices to add to the batter: 1 tsp ground cinnamon or nutmeg

Instructions

Combine flour, ground flaxseeds, milk and egg and whisk or blend until smooth. Let the batter sit for about 2-3 minutes.

Warm the oil in a non-stick frying pan over medium heat. Spoon ¼ cup batter into the pan and cook for 2 to 3 minutes or until bubbles appear on the surface. Turn the pancake over and cook the other side for 1 to 2 minutes or until golden and cooked through. Transfer the pancake to a plate and cover to keep warm. Repeat with the remaining batter to make 3 pancakes.

Top the pancakes with the sliced banana and some honey or maple syrup to taste.

·idge (Oatmeal) with Banana, Cinnamon, Almonds & Coconut Milk – Week 1

Serves: 1

Ingredients

½ cup rolled oats
1 tbsp raw almonds, sliced
1 tsp ground cinnamon
1 banana, sliced
1 cup coconut milk* (unsweetened)
Drizzle of honey or maple syrup – *optional*

Instructions

Prepare and cook the oats according to the package directions. Once the oats are cooked, stir in the almonds and cinnamon. Top with the banana slices and pour the coconut milk over the porridge, and serve. Add a drizzle of honey or maple syrup, if you like.

* can be substituted with almond milk, normal cow's milk or any other milk you prefer.

Porridge (Oatmeal) with Banana, Cinnamon, Almonds & Coconut Milk + Flaxseeds or Walnuts – Week 2-5

Serves: 1

Ingredients

- ½ cup rolled oats
- 1 tbsp ground flaxseeds or some walnuts, roughly chopped
- 1 tbsp raw almonds, sliced
- 1 tsp ground cinnamon
- 1 banana, sliced
- 1 cup coconut milk* (unsweetened)
- Drizzle of honey or maple syrup – *optional*

Instructions

Prepare and cook the oats according to the package directions. Once the oats are cooked, stir in the ground flaxseeds or walnuts, almonds and cinnamon. Top with the banana slices and pour the coconut milk over the porridge, and serve. Add a drizzle of honey or maple syrup, if you like.

* can be substituted with almond milk, normal cow's milk or any other milk you prefer.

Quinoa Porridge (Oatmeal) with Banana, Cinnamon and Almonds – Week 1

Serves: 1

Ingredients

½ cup quinoa
½ cup water
½ cup of milk (your choice of dairy, almond, coconut milk, etc.)
1 tsp ground cinnamon
1 tbsp sliced raw almonds
1 banana, sliced
1-2 tbsps berries (frozen or fresh) – *optional*
Drizzle of honey or maple syrup

Instructions

Rinse the quinoa well under cold, running water. Then combine with the water in a pot and bring to the boil. Reduce to medium heat – cover and cook for about 10 minutes until soft. Add the milk, cinnamon and honey (or maple syrup) and simmer gently for 5 minutes. Once the quinoa is cooked, stir in the sliced raw almonds. Top with banana slices and berries, and serve.

Quinoa Porridge (Oatmeal) with Banana, Cinnamon and Almonds + Flaxseeds or Walnuts – Week 2-5

Serves: 1

Ingredients

½ cup quinoa
½ cup water
½ cup of milk (your choice of dairy, almond, coconut milk, etc.)
1 tsp ground cinnamon
1 tbsp sliced raw almonds
1 tbsp ground flaxseeds or some walnuts, roughly chopped
1 banana, sliced
1-2 tbsps berries (frozen or fresh) – *optional*
Drizzle of honey or maple syrup

Instructions

Rinse the quinoa well under cold, running water. Then combine with the water in a pot and bring to the boil. Reduce to medium heat – cover and cook for about 10 minutes until soft. Add the milk, cinnamon and honey (or maple syrup) and simmer gently for 5 minutes. Once the quinoa is cooked, stir in the sliced raw almonds and ground flaxseeds or walnuts. Top with banana slices and berries, and serve.

Spinach and Mushroom Scrambled Eggs

Serves: 1

Ingredients

2 eggs
2 cups baby spinach (fresh)
½ cup button mushrooms, sliced
1 tbsp olive oil (preferably extra virgin olive oil)
Salt and pepper, to taste

Instructions

Beat the eggs in a small bowl and set aside. Heat the olive oil in a non-stick pan over medium-high heat. Then add the mushrooms. Cook them for about 3 to 4 minutes or until tender and lightly browned, stirring occasionally. Add the spinach and cook for 1-2 minutes or until the spinach has wilted. Reduce the heat to medium and add the eggs. Cook and stir until the eggs are thickened. Season with salt and pepper.

Serve with some wholemeal/ wholegrain toast.

Spinach and Poached Egg Toast

Serves: 1

Ingredients

2 eggs
2 slices of bread (preferably wholegrain or wholemeal bread)
1 tbsp olive oil (preferably extra virgin olive oil)
1 cup baby spinach
1 garlic clove, peeled and crushed - *optional*
1 tsp lemon juice - *optional*
Pepper, to taste

Instructions

Bring a saucepan of water to a rolling boil. Break one egg at a time and carefully slide it into the boiling water. Put a lid on the saucepan and turn off the heat. Leave the eggs to cook in the hot water for 3 minutes.

In the meantime, toast your 2 slices of bread. Warm the olive oil in another saucepan over a medium heat. Add the crushed garlic and lemon juice. Then add the spinach to the warm olive oil, stir well and heat through for 1-2 minutes or until the spinach has wilted.

To serve, place a bed of spinach on each slice of toast, pop the poached egg on top and sprinkle with some black pepper.

Note: Of course, you can substitute the poached eggs with fried or scrambled eggs.

Mid-morning Snacks

Banana and Almond Smoothie

Serves: 1

Ingredients

1 cup almond milk (unsweetened)
1 banana, sliced and frozen*

Instructions

Place the ingredients in a blender and blend until smooth.

* Freeze peeled and sliced ripe bananas for easier blending.

Banana and Almond Smoothie with Spirulina

Serves: 1

Ingredients

1 cup almond milk (unsweetened)
½ tsp - 1 tsp Spirulina (organic Spirulina powder)
1 banana, sliced and frozen*

Instructions

Place the frozen banana slices, then the Spirulina powder and the almond milk in a blender and blend until smooth.

* Freeze peeled and sliced ripe bananas for easier blending.

Banana and Greens Smoothie

Serves: 1

Ingredients

1 cup filtered water or coconut water
2 cups fresh spinach or other dark leafy greens (stems removed)
1 banana, sliced and frozen*
Juice of ½ lemon

Instructions

Place the frozen banana slices, then the spinach, lemon juice and the water in a blender and blend until smooth.

* Freeze peeled and sliced ripe bananas for easier blending.

Banana and Greens Smoothie with Spirulina

Serves: 1

Ingredients

1 cup filtered water or coconut water
½ tsp - 1 tsp Spirulina (organic Spirulina powder)
2 cups fresh spinach or other dark leafy greens (stems removed)
1 banana, sliced and frozen*
Juice of ½ lemon

Instructions

Place the frozen banana slices, then the spinach, Spirulina powder, lemon juice and water in a blender and blend until smooth.

* Freeze peeled and sliced ripe bananas for easier blending.

Banana and Greens Smoothie with Spirulina and Berries

Serves: 1

Ingredients

- 1 cup filtered water or coconut water
- ½ tsp - 1 tsp Spirulina (organic Spirulina powder)
- 2 cups fresh spinach or other dark leafy greens (stems removed)
- 1 cup berries (fresh or frozen) - e.g. strawberries, raspberries, blueberries, etc.
- 1 banana, sliced and frozen*
- Juice of ½ lemon

Instructions

Place the frozen banana slices, then the berries, spinach, Spirulina powder, lemon juice and water in a blender and blend until smooth.

* Freeze peeled and sliced ripe bananas for easier blending.

Chocolate-Chia Smoothie

Serves: 1

Ingredients

> 1 cup coconut milk (unsweetened)
> ½ cup filtered water
> 1 tbsp raw cacao powder (unsweetened)
> 1 tbsp chia seeds
> 1 tsp ground cinnamon
> 1 banana, sliced and frozen*

Instructions

Place the frozen banana slices, then the coconut milk, chia seeds, cacao powder, ground cinnamon and water in a blender and blend until smooth.

* Freeze peeled and sliced ripe bananas for easier blending.

Green Smoothie with Flaxseed

Serves: 1

Ingredients

- 1 cup almond milk (unsweetened)
- 1 tbsp ground flaxseed
- 2 cups fresh spinach or other dark leafy greens (stems removed)
- 1 banana, sliced and frozen*

Instructions

Place the frozen banana slices, then the spinach, ground flaxseed and almond milk in a blender and blend until smooth.

* Freeze peeled and sliced ripe bananas for easier blending.

Green Smoothie with Flaxseed and Berries

Serves: 1

Ingredients

- 1 cup almond milk (unsweetened)
- 1 tbsp ground flaxseed
- 2 cups fresh spinach or other dark leafy greens (stems removed)
- 1 cup berries (fresh or frozen) - e.g. strawberries, raspberries, blueberries, etc.
- 1 banana, sliced and frozen*

Instructions

Place the frozen banana slices, then the berries, spinach, ground flaxseed and almond milk in a blender and blend until smooth.

* Freeze peeled and sliced ripe bananas for easier blending.

Lunches

Broccoli Soup

Serves: 1

Ingredients

1 broccoli head, cut into florets and stalks shredded
1 garlic clove, crushed
1 cup chicken stock
¼ cup cream
Salt and pepper, to taste

Instructions

Put the broccoli, garlic and chicken stock in a saucepan and cook until the broccoli softens. Season with salt and pepper and add the cream. Then pour everything in a blender or use a stick blender and blend until smooth. Enjoy with some wholegrain toast on the side if you like.

Chicken Avocado Sandwich

Serves: 1

Ingredients

2 slices of bread (preferably wholegrain or wholemeal bread)
1 cup barbeque chicken, shredded or 2 slices chicken deli meat
½ medium-sized avocado, skin and seed removed
Juice of ½ lemon
Salt and pepper, to taste

Instructions

Mash the avocado in a small bowl and combine with lemon juice, some salt and pepper.

Spread the avocado mash evenly onto the 2 slices of bread (fresh or toasted). Top one slice of bread with the chicken and place the other slice on top.

Chicken Sandwich with Apple, Walnut and Spinach

Serves: 1

Ingredients

- 2 slices of bread (preferably wholegrain or wholemeal bread)
- 1 cup barbeque or cooked chicken, shredded or 2 slices chicken deli meat
- 2 tsps mayonnaise
- ¼ cup apple (e.g. Granny Smith), finely sliced or grated
- 1 tbsp walnuts, chopped
- ½ cup fresh baby spinach leaves

Instructions

Spread the mayonnaise evenly onto the 2 slices of bread (fresh or toasted). Layer the chicken, apple, walnuts and spinach leaves on one of the bread slices and place the remaining bread slice on top.

Chicken Sandwich with Avocado, Brie Cheese and Spinach

Serves: 1

Ingredients

- 2 slices of bread (preferably wholegrain or wholemeal)
- 1 cup barbeque chicken, shredded or 2 slices chicken deli meat (preferably organic and nitrate-free)
- 4 slices of brie cheese (or any cheese you prefer)
- ½ medium-sized avocado, skin and seed removed
- ½ cup fresh baby spinach leaves

Instructions

Spread the avocado evenly onto the 2 slices of bread (fresh or toasted). Layer the chicken, brie cheese slices and spinach leaves on one of the bread slices and place the remaining bread slice on top.

Cream Cheese, Black Olive, Walnut and Spinach Sandwich

Serves: 1

Ingredients

- 2 slices of bread (preferably wholegrain or wholemeal bread)
- 2 tbsps cream cheese
- 2 tbsps black olives, chopped
- 1 tbsp walnuts, chopped
- ½ cup fresh baby spinach leaves

Instructions

Spread the cream cheese onto 2 slices of bread (fresh or toasted). Layer the black olives onto 1 slice of bread and sprinkle the walnuts on top. Add the spinach leaves and place the other slice of bread on top.

Grilled Chicken Breast with Avocado and Spinach Salad

Serves: 1

Ingredients

1 boneless, skinless chicken breast, grilled
1 cup fresh baby spinach leaves
½ medium-sized avocado, skin and seed removed & cut in cubes
4 cherry tomatoes, halved
Juice of ¼ lemon
Salt and pepper, to taste

Instructions

Mix the spinach leaves, avocado cubes and tomato halves and arrange on a serving plate. Drizzle the lemon juice on top and season with salt and pepper.

Add the grilled chicken breast to the plate and serve.

Grilled Chicken Breast with Avocado, Spinach and Walnut Salad

Serves: 1

Ingredients

1 boneless, skinless chicken breast, grilled
1 tbsp walnuts, roughly chopped
1 cup fresh baby spinach leaves
½ medium-sized avocado, skin and seed removed & cut in cubes
Juice of ¼ lemon
Salt and pepper, to taste

Instructions

Put the walnuts into a small frying pan. Cook over medium heat for 3 to 4 minutes or until the walnuts are golden and roasted while shaking the frying pan often.

Mix the spinach leaves and avocado cubes and arrange on a serving plate. Drizzle the lemon juice on top and season with salt and pepper. Top the salad off with the roasted walnuts.

Add the grilled chicken breast to the plate and serve.

Grilled Chicken Breast with Spinach, Walnut and Feta Salad

Serves: 1

Ingredients

- 1 boneless, skinless chicken breast, grilled
- 1 cup fresh baby spinach leaves
- ½ cup Lebanese cucumber, cut in cubes
- 1 orange, peeled and segmented*
- 1 tbsp walnuts, roughly chopped and toasted**
- 2 tbsps feta cheese, crumbled
- 2 tbsps balsamic vinegar

Instructions

* To segment the orange, remove the peel and white pith. Use a sharp knife to cut down either side of the membrane to release segments.

** Put the walnuts into a small frying pan. Cook over medium heat for 3 to 4 minutes or until the walnuts are golden and roasted while shaking the frying pan often.

Place spinach leaves, cucumber cubes, orange segments, walnuts and feta cheese in a bowl. Add the balsamic vinegar and toss gently to combine.

Arrange the salad and grilled chicken breast on a serving plate and enjoy.

Ham, Cheese and Spinach Sandwich

Serves: 1

Ingredients

2 slices of bread (preferably wholegrain or wholemeal bread)
2 slices of your favourite sliced ham
1-2 slices of Swiss cheese
½ cup fresh baby spinach leaves
2 tsps butter

Instructions

Butter your 2 slices of bread (fresh or toasted). Then add the ham and Swiss cheese on 1 slice of bread. Add the spinach leaves and place the other slice of bread on top.

Ham Sandwich with Avocado Spread

Serves: 1

Ingredients

2 slices of bread (preferably wholegrain or wholemeal bread)
2 slices of your favourite sliced ham
1 avocado, skin and seed removed
Juice of ¼ lemon
Drizzle of olive oil (preferably extra virgin olive oil)
Salt and pepper, to taste

Instructions

In a small bowl, mash the avocado and combine with lemon juice, olive oil, salt and pepper.

Cover the 2 slices of bread (fresh or toasted) with the avocado spread. Top one slice of bread with the ham and place the other slice of bread on top.

Optional: Garnish with some tomato or cucumber slices.

Open-Faced Avocado Sandwich

Serves: 1

Ingredients

2 slices of bread (preferably wholegrain or wholemeal bread)
1 avocado, skin and seed removed
Juice of ½ lemon
Drizzle of olive oil (preferably extra virgin olive oil)
Salt and pepper, to taste

Instructions

Spread the avocado evenly onto the 2 slices of bread (fresh or toasted). Drizzle some lemon juice onto the avocado and sprinkle with some salt and pepper. Drizzle a little bit of olive oil on top.

Optional: Garnish with some tomato or cucumber slices.

Open-Faced Avocado Sandwich with Feta Cheese

Serves: 1

Ingredients

2 slices of bread (preferably wholegrain or wholemeal bread)
1 avocado, skin and seed removed
2 tbsps feta cheese
Juice of ½ lemon
Drizzle of olive oil (preferably extra virgin olive oil)
Pepper, to taste

Instructions

In a bowl, mix together the avocado, feta cheese and lemon juice. Spread the avocado mash evenly onto the 2 slices of bread (fresh or toasted). Serve with a sprinkle of pepper and a drizzle of olive oil.

Quinoa Salad with Avocado and Tomatoes

Serves: 2-3

Ingredients

½ cup quinoa
1 cup cherry tomatoes, halved
1 avocado, skin and seed removed & cut in cubes
2 tbsps lemon juice
¼ cup parsley, roughly chopped - *optional*
1 cup fresh baby spinach leaves - *optional*
½ cup cucumber, diced - *optional*
2 tbsps red onion, diced - *optional*
Salt and pepper, to taste

Instructions

Prepare and cook the quinoa according to package instructions.

Let the quinoa cool. Add all the ingredients to a bowl and toss well.

Note: This salad should last 3-4 days in the fridge.

Roast Beef, Cheese and Spinach Sandwich

Serves: 1

Ingredients

> 2 slices of bread (preferably wholegrain, wholemeal or rye bread)
> 2 slices roast beef – deli or cut from your own roast
> 1-2 slices of Cheddar cheese
> ½ cup fresh baby spinach leaves
> 2 tsps Dijon mustard
> 2 tsps butter

Instructions

Butter the 2 slices of bread (fresh or toasted) and spread on the Dijon mustard. Then add the roast beef and Cheddar cheese on 1 slice of bread. Add the spinach leaves and place the other slice of bread on top.

Smoked Salmon Sandwich with Cream Cheese, Capers and Spinach

Serves: 1

Ingredients

2 slices of bread (preferably wholegrain or wholemeal bread)
2 slices of smoked salmon, thinly sliced
2 tbsps cream cheese
1 tsp capers, drained
½ cup fresh baby spinach leaves
Pepper, to taste – *optional*

Instructions

Spread the cream cheese evenly onto the 2 slices of bread (fresh or toasted). Layer the smoked salmon slices and spinach leaves on one of the bread slices and sprinkle with capers. Season with pepper and top with the remaining bread slice. Garnish with some slices of red onion and a slice of lime – *optional*.

Tuna Quinoa Salad

Serves: 1

Ingredients

½ cup quinoa
1 small can (95g) tuna in spring water, drained and broken into
  chunks
¼ cup cherry tomatoes, halved
¼ cup cucumber, diced
¼ red onion, finely diced
½ tbsp olive oil (preferably extra virgin olive oil)
1 tbsp lemon juice
¼ tsp salt
1 pinch ground black pepper, or to taste

Instructions

Prepare and cook the quinoa according to package instructions.

Transfer the quinoa to a bowl and allow to cool. Add tuna,
tomatoes, cucumber and onion to the bowl and combine.

To make the salad dressing, whisk together the lemon juice, olive oil,
salt and pepper in a separate bowl. Add the dressing to the quinoa
salad bowl and toss well.

Turkey Sandwich with Avocado, Brie Cheese, Cranberry Sauce and Spinach

Serves: 1

Ingredients

2 slices of bread (preferably wholegrain or wholemeal bread)
2 turkey deli meat slices (preferably organic and nitrate-free) or cooked turkey slices
4 slices of brie cheese (or any cheese you prefer)
1 tbsp cranberry sauce
¼ medium-sized avocado, skin and seed removed
½ cup fresh baby spinach leaves

Instructions

Spread the avocado evenly onto 1 slice of bread (fresh or toasted). Layer the spinach leaves, brie cheese slices and the turkey on top. Spread the cranberry sauce onto the other bread slice and place on top of the turkey, sauce-side down.

Turkey Sandwich with Avocado, Spinach and Tomato

Serves: 1

Ingredients

- 2 slices of bread (preferably wholegrain or wholemeal bread)
- 2 turkey deli meat slices (preferably organic and nitrate-free) or cooked turkey slices
- ½ avocado, skin and seed removed
- ½ cup fresh baby spinach leaves
- 1 spring onion (scallion), trimmed and finely chopped (or 1 small sliced red onion to taste)
- 1 tomato, sliced
- 1 tsp wholegrain mustard – *optional*

Instructions

Spread the avocado flesh evenly onto the 2 slices of bread (fresh or toasted). Layer the spinach and turkey on one of the bread slices and top with spring onion, tomato and mustard. Sandwich together and enjoy!

Warm Lentil, Quinoa and Spinach Salad

Serves: 1

Ingredients

¼ cup lentils
¼ cup quinoa (or wild rice)
1 cup fresh baby spinach leaves
½ cup green capsicum (bell pepper), sliced
1 spring onion (scallion), sliced
1 tsp olive oil (preferably extra virgin olive oil)
Pepper, to taste

Instructions

Separately, cook the lentils and quinoa according to the package directions.

The spinach leaves will be steamed. Select a pot with a lid and put the spinach in it. Add about 2 tablespoons of water to the bottom of the pot and put the lid on the pot. Place the pot over a low heat, so that the spinach will cook gently. This should take about five minutes. The spinach is finished cooking when it is bright green and limp. Then drain the cooked spinach in a colander to remove excess water. Put the spinach on a plate.

Spoon the warm quinoa and lentils over the steamed spinach. Top with the capsicum, spring onion, olive oil and pepper.

Mid-afternoon Snacks

Cacao and Almond Bliss Balls

Makes approximately 8 bliss balls

Ingredients

1 cup raw almonds
1 cup dates (pitted)
4 tbsps warm water, to mix
2 tbsps raw cacao powder (unsweetened)
2 tbsps desiccated coconut - *optional*
Optional: goji berries, chia seeds, "superfood" powders such as Spirulina or Maca

Instructions

Place all of the ingredients in a food processor, except for the water and the dates. Blend on a low speed to begin with and then on high once the mixture starts to move properly in the food processor. Then add the dates, a couple at a time, until everything is mixed well. Add the water to the mixture and blend again.

Use a tablespoon to measure out the mixture for each bliss ball and roll it into walnut size balls.

Additionally, you can roll the bliss balls in coatings such as desiccated coconut, sesame seeds or chia seeds.

Store in the refrigerator.

Dinners

Chicken and Broccoli Stir-Fry with Rice/ Brown Rice

Serves: 1

Ingredients

1 cup broccoli (can be substituted with Asian greens such as bok choy or Chinese broccoli)
1 boneless, skinless chicken breast, diced
1 tbsp ginger, finely sliced
1 garlic clove, finely chopped/minced
1 red onion, sliced
1 tbsp olive oil
½ tbsp soy sauce (preferably MSG-free soy sauce) or *Soy Sauce Substitute* (→ see **Sauces**)
½ tbsp honey
⅓ cup rice (use brown rice in Week 4)
½ tsp red chili pepper, finely sliced/chopped or ½ tsp mild chili powder (optional)
Salt and pepper, to taste

Instructions

Cook the rice according to the package instructions. Start with the rice well before the other steps as it takes longer to cook.

Shred the broccoli into small bite-size pieces and boil in salted water for 4-6 minutes, or until tender.

Heat the olive oil in a non-stick wok or frypan (skillet) and stir-fry the ginger, garlic, onion and chili for about 2 minutes. If you are using chili powder, stir it in only briefly after stir-frying the ginger, garlic and onion. Then add the chicken and stir-fry until chicken starts to turn golden brown. Drain the broccoli and reserve about 2 tbsps of the broccoli cooking water. Add the broccoli, broccoli water (2 tbsps), soy sauce and honey to the wok/frypan (skillet) and cook until heated through. Add some pepper, if you like.
Arrange the rice and chicken & broccoli stir-fry on a plate and serve.

Grilled Chicken with Mashed Potatoes and Broccoli

Serves: 1

Ingredients

1 boneless, skinless chicken breast, grilled
2 medium-sized potatoes, peeled and cut into quarters
1 cup broccoli, cut into florets
¼ cup warm milk or cream
½ tbsp flaxseed oil
Salt and pepper, to taste

Instructions

Boil the peeled and quartered potatoes in a saucepan of lightly salted water. Cook the potatoes for about 20 minutes or until they are soft enough to mash. Drain them thoroughly and push the potato pieces through a ricer into a bowl (or use a potato masher). Add the warm milk, flaxseed oil, some salt and pepper to the mashed potatoes and mix together with a wooden spoon.

Meanwhile, steam the broccoli. Put the broccoli florets into a steamer set over a pan of boiling water or if you don't have a steamer, put the broccoli florets in a pot and add a small amount of water so that the broccoli is only half covered. Cover the pot with a lid and place it on the stove and heat to medium high. Allow the broccoli to steam for about 5-10 minutes. The broccoli is finished steaming when it looks bright green and a fork slides into it easily.

Arrange the grilled chicken, mashed potatoes and steamed broccoli on a plate and serve.

Grilled Fish with Quinoa Salad

Serves: 1

Ingredients

1 fish fillet (e.g. salmon, snapper or other white fish), grilled
½ cup quinoa
½ cup cherry tomatoes, halved
½ cup cucumber, diced
½ avocado, cut in cubes
1 tbsp lemon juice
Sea salt, to taste

Instructions

Prepare and cook the quinoa according to package instructions.

Let the quinoa cool. Add all the ingredients to a bowl and toss well.

Arrange half of the quinoa salad and the grilled fish fillet on a plate and serve. Save the other half of the quinoa salad covered in the fridge for lunch the next day.

Ground Beef-Stuffed Capsicum (Bell Pepper) with Quinoa

Serves: 1

Ingredients

½ cup quinoa
100g (¼ lbs) ground beef
1 green capsicum (bell pepper)
1 egg
¼ onion, chopped
1 tbsp olive oil (preferably extra virgin olive oil)
1 tbsp tomato paste
Salt and pepper, to taste

Instructions

Prepare and cook the quinoa according to package instructions.

Remove the pulp and the seeds from the capsicum by cutting out the stem from the top and carefully lifting the pulp out. Remove all of the seeds by rinsing the inside with water.

Combine the ground beef, egg and chopped onion as well as salt and pepper in a bowl. Stuff the capsicum with the beef mixture.

Add the olive to a non-stick frypan/skillet (make sure you have a lid for it) and preheat over medium-high heat for 2 minutes. Place the stuffed capsicum in the frypan (skillet) and let the outside brown slightly. Make sure you turn the capsicum on all of the sides, including top and bottom, to brown evenly. Meanwhile, put some water in a kettle and let it boil. As soon as the capsicum is browned evenly, add 2 cups of boiling water to the frypan (skillet). Then add the tomato paste to the water and stir to combine. Season the tomato sauce with salt and pepper. Reduce the heat, cover the frypan (skillet) with a lid and cook for about 30-40 minutes. Check occasionally, if sauce has reduced too much, add additional boiling water, salt and pepper, if required.

Place the stuffed capsicum with the tomato sauce and quinoa on a plate and serve.

Ground Turkey-Stuffed Capsicum (Bell Pepper) with Quinoa

Serves: 1

Ingredients

½ cup quinoa
100g (3.5 oz/ ¼ lbs) ground turkey
1 green capsicum (bell pepper)
1 egg
¼ onion, chopped
1 tbsp olive oil (preferably extra virgin olive oil)
1 tbsp tomato paste
Salt and pepper, to taste

Instructions

Prepare and cook the quinoa according to package instructions.

Remove the pulp and the seeds from the capsicum by cutting out the stem from the top and carefully lifting the pulp out. Remove all of the seeds by rinsing the inside with water.

Combine the ground turkey, egg and chopped onion as well as salt and pepper in a bowl. Stuff the capsicum with the turkey mixture.

Add the olive to a non-stick frypan/skillet (make sure you have a lid for it) and preheat over medium-high heat for 2 minutes. Place the stuffed capsicum in the frypan (skillet) and let the outside brown slightly. Make sure you turn the capsicum on all of the sides, including top and bottom, to brown evenly. Meanwhile, put some water in a kettle and let it boil. As soon as the capsicum is browned evenly, add 2 cups of boiling water to the frypan (skillet). Then add the tomato paste to the water and stir to combine. Season the tomato sauce with salt and pepper. Reduce the heat, cover the frypan (skillet) with a lid and cook for about 30-40 minutes. Check occasionally, if sauce has reduced too much, add additional boiling water, salt and pepper, if required.

Place the stuffed capsicum with the tomato sauce and quinoa on a plate and serve.

Ground Turkey with Brown Rice, Spinach and Mushrooms

Serves: 1

Ingredients

100g (3.5 oz/ ¼ lbs) ground turkey
⅓ cup brown rice
1 cup fresh baby spinach
1 cup button mushrooms, sliced
1 tbsp olive oil (preferably extra virgin olive oil)
½ cup tinned diced tomatoes
1 garlic clove, crushed
¼ onion, chopped
Salt and pepper, to taste

Instructions

Cook rice according to package instructions.

In a heated frypan (skillet), add olive oil and sauté the onion and garlic. Add the ground turkey and cook over medium heat. Once the turkey is cooked through, add the tomatoes, mushrooms and fresh spinach. Cover and cook until spinach is completely wilted and mushrooms have softened. Season with salt and pepper, to taste. Serve over the rice and enjoy!

Ground Turkey with Rice and Spinach

Serves: 1

Ingredients

100g (3.5 oz/ ¼ lbs) ground turkey
⅓ cup rice (you can also use quinoa)
1 cup fresh baby spinach leaves
1 tbsp olive oil (preferably extra virgin olive oil)
½ cup tinned diced tomatoes
1 garlic clove, crushed
¼ onion, chopped
Salt and pepper, to taste

Instructions

Cook rice according to package instructions.

In a heated frypan (skillet), add olive oil and sauté the onion and garlic. Add the ground turkey and cook over medium heat. Once the turkey is cooked through, add the tomatoes and fresh spinach. Cover and cook until spinach is completely wilted. Season with salt and pepper to taste. Serve over the rice and enjoy!

Pan-Seared Salmon with Lentil and Quinoa Salad

Serves: 1

Ingredients

1 salmon fillet
¼ cup quinoa
¼ cup tinned brown lentils, washed and drained
1 tbsp olive oil (preferably extra virgin olive oil) for salad
1 tbsp olive oil (preferably extra virgin olive oil) for salmon
1 tbsp lemon juice
½ tsp Dijon mustard
½ spring onion (scallion), chopped
A few fresh coriander/cilantro leaves, chopped (optional)
1 lemon wedge, to garnish
Salt and pepper, to taste

Instructions

Cook the quinoa according to the package directions. When cooked, remove from the heat, fluff with a fork and leave uncovered.

In a small bowl, whisk the mustard and lemon juice together, and drizzle in the olive oil to make an emulsion. Add salt and pepper, to taste.

Preheat a non-stick frypan (skillet) over medium heat for 3 minutes. Coat the salmon with olive oil, place in the pre-warmed frypan (skillet) and increase heat to high. Cook for 3 minutes. Sprinkle with some salt and pepper. Turn salmon over and cook for 5 minutes, or until browned. Transfer the salmon to a serving plate and garnish with a lemon wedge.

To assemble the salad, mix the quinoa, lentils, spring onion and chopped coriander. Top with the dressing and toss to combine. Add the salad to the plate and serve.

Pan-Seared Salmon with Lentil and Spinach Salad

Serves: 1

Ingredients

1 salmon fillet
2 baby potatoes, washed, unpeeled
¼ cup tinned brown lentils, washed and drained
½ cup fresh baby spinach
4 cherry tomatoes, quartered
1 spring onion (scallion) - including green tops, end trimmed, chopped
¼ cup parsley, chopped
1 tbsp olive oil (preferably extra virgin olive oil)
1 tsp lemon juice
1 tsp wholegrain mustard
1 lemon wedge, to garnish
Salt and pepper, to taste

Instructions

Place the unpeeled potatoes in a saucepan and cover with water. Bring to the boil and allow to simmer for about 10 minutes or until they can be pierced easily with a knife. Drain and set aside.

Meanwhile, combine the lentils, spinach, tomatoes, spring onions and parsley in a bowl.

In a separate small bowl, combine the lemon juice and mustard to make a dressing for the salad. Mix the dressing through the lentil and spinach salad.

Preheat a non-stick frypan (skillet) over medium heat for 3 minutes. Coat the salmon with olive oil, place in the frypan (skillet) and increase heat to high. Cook for 3 minutes. Sprinkle with some salt and pepper. Turn salmon over and cook for 5 minutes, or until browned. Transfer the salmon to a serving plate and garnish with a lemon wedge. Add the potatoes and lentil and spinach salad to the plate and serve.

Pan-Seared Turkey Cutlets with Roast Potatoes and Broccoli

Serves: 1

Ingredients

1-2 turkey cutlets
2 tbsps olive oil (preferably extra virgin olive oil)
2 medium-sized potatoes (you can also use 1 medium-sized sweet
   potato instead), peeled and diced (about 1cm thick cubes)
1 cup broccoli, cut into florets
Drizzle of flaxseed oil
Salt and pepper, to taste

Instructions

Preheat the oven to 230°C (450°F). Line a roasting pan with non-stick baking paper. Toss the potato cubes in about 1 tbsp of olive oil. Season with salt and pepper and spread in the pan. Roast for about 30 minutes.

Heat the remaining olive oil in a frying pan or cast iron skillet over high heat. Season the turkey cutlets with some salt and pepper and place into the hot pan. Cook them for a few minutes on each side until they are nicely browned on the outside and fully cooked and opaque on the inside. Remove from the pan and rest the cutlets at room temperature for a few minutes before serving.

Meanwhile, steam the broccoli. Put the broccoli florets into a steamer set over a pan of boiling water or if you don't have a steamer, put the broccoli florets in a pot and add a small amount of water so that the broccoli is only half covered. Cover the pot with a lid and place it on the stove and heat to medium high. Allow the broccoli to steam for about 5-10 minutes. The broccoli is finished steaming when it looks bright green and a fork slides into it easily.

Arrange the turkey cutlets, roast potatoes and broccoli on a plate. Drizzle some flaxseed oil over the steamed broccoli and serve.

Pasta with Broccoli and Pine Nuts

Serves: 1

Ingredients

⅔ cup dry penne pasta
1 cup broccoli, shredded into bite-size pieces
2 tbsps pine nuts, toasted
2 tsps olive oil (preferably extra virgin olive oil)
1 garlic glove, minced or thinly sliced
Parmesan cheese, grated to garnish
Salt and pepper, to taste

Instructions

Cook the pasta according to the package directions.

Boil the shredded broccoli in salted water for 4-6 minutes, or until tender. Reserve about 2 tablespoons of the broccoli cooking water and drain the rest. Add the pine nuts, olive oil and garlic to the broccoli and mix in the reserved water. Mix with the cooked and drained pasta, and serve warm with grated parmesan cheese on top and seasoned to taste.

Pork with Sweet Potato Chips and Wilted Spinach

Serves: 1

Ingredients

200g (7 oz/ ½ lbs) pork loin steak or 300g (10.5 oz/ ⅔ lbs) pork loin cutlet (bone-in)
1 medium sweet potato, peeled and cut to resemble chips or cut lengthwise into wedges
2 cups of fresh baby spinach leaves
2 tbsps olive oil (preferably extra virgin olive oil)
Salt and pepper, to taste

Instructions

Pre heat fan-forced oven to 200°C (400°F). In a mixing bowl, toss sweet potato with 1 tbsp olive oil, salt and pepper. Transfer to a baking tray lined with a non-stick baking sheet and bake in the oven for about 20 minutes until cooked through, turning occasionally.

Meanwhile, heat the remaining 1 tbsp of olive oil in a non-stick frying pan over medium-high heat. Season the pork with salt and pepper on both sides and cook for about 4-5 minutes each side or until golden brown and cooked through. Transfer to a plate and let the pork rest for 5 minutes.

Return the same frying pan to medium heat and add the spinach. Cook the spinach for about 1 to 2 minutes or until just wilted.

Arrange the pork, sweet potato chips and spinach on a plate and serve.

Quinoa Stir-Fry with Vegetables and Chicken

Serves: 1

Ingredients

¼ cup quinoa
1 boneless, skinless chicken breast, diced
1 tbsp olive oil (preferably extra virgin olive oil)
1 small carrot, finely diced
¼ cup frozen peas
½ tsp ginger, grated
1 garlic clove, finely chopped/minced
½ tbsp soy sauce (preferably MSG-free soy sauce) or Soy Sauce
  Substitute (→ see **Sauces**)
1 egg, beaten
½ spring onion (scallion), chopped
½ tsp red chili pepper, finely chopped (optional)
Salt and pepper, to taste

Instructions

Prepare and cook the quinoa according to package instructions.
When cooked, remove from the heat, fluff with a fork and leave
uncovered.

Heat the olive oil in a wok or frypan (skillet) over medium-high heat.
Add the carrot and cook until tender. Then add ginger, garlic and
chili, and cook for about 2 minutes, stirring frequently. Add the
chicken pieces and cook until they are lightly browned, stirring
frequently. Then add peas and cook until heated through, stirring
frequently. Remove chicken and vegetables and put aside. Return
wok/frypan (skillet) to heat and add the quinoa and egg. Cook for
about 2 minutes, stirring constantly to combine the egg with the
quinoa. Then return vegetables and chicken to the wok/frypan
(skillet) and add spring onion and soy sauce, salt and pepper. Stir
together and serve.

Spaghetti with Spinach and Garlic

Serves: 1

Ingredients

50g (2 oz/ 1/10 lbs) dry spaghetti (or ⅔ cup dry penne or spiral pasta)
2 cups fresh baby spinach
2 tbsps olive oil (preferably extra virgin olive oil)
1 garlic clove, minced or thinly sliced
Parmesan cheese, grated to garnish
Salt and pepper, to taste

Instructions

Cook the pasta according to the package directions. Drain and set aside, reserving about 4 tablespoons of the cooking water.

While the pasta is cooking, combine the olive oil and garlic in a frypan (skillet) over medium heat. Cook for 4 to 6 minutes, stirring often until the garlic becomes fragrant and is beginning to turn golden. Then add the spinach and some salt and pepper. Cook for about 2 minutes until the spinach begins to wilt. Add the drained pasta and 2 tablespoons of the reserved cooking water. Cook for 1 to 2 minutes, tossing and stirring until everything is combined. (If the pasta isn't tender or seems dry, add the remainder of the reserved cooking water and continue to cook and stir until done.)

Season to taste with salt and pepper and serve with some grated parmesan cheese on top.

Steak with Broccoli and Baked Potato with Sour Cream

Serves: 1

Ingredients

1 scotch fillet or porterhouse steak
2 tbsps olive oil (preferably extra virgin olive oil)
1 large potato, washed, unpeeled
2 tbsps sour cream
1 cup broccoli, cut into florets
Drizzle of flaxseed oil
Salt and pepper, to taste

Instructions

Preheat the oven to 220°C (425°F). Rub the potato with olive oil and sprinkle with salt and pepper. Then prick the potato with the tines of a fork. Place the potato directly on the oven rack or on a baking sheet. (You can also wrap the potato in tin foil and bake on the grill over high heat.) Cook for 45 to 60 minutes until the potato skin is crispy and there is no resistance when sticking it with a fork. Let the potato cool for several minutes. Before serving, crack the baked potato open by creating a dotted line from end to end with a fork and then squeeze the ends towards one another. Top with sour cream.

Heat the remaining olive oil in a frying pan over medium-high heat. Season the steak with some salt and pepper. Add steak to the frying pan and cook for about 3 minutes on each side or according to your preference. Remove from the pan and rest the steak covered at room temperature for at least 5 minutes.

Meanwhile, steam the broccoli. Put the broccoli florets into a steamer set over a pan of boiling water or if you don't have a steamer, put the broccoli florets in a pot and add a small amount of water so that the broccoli is only half covered. Cover the pot with a lid and place it on the stove and heat to medium high. Allow the broccoli to steam for about 5-10 minutes. The broccoli is finished steaming when it looks bright green and a fork slides into it easily.

Arrange the steak, baked potato and broccoli on a plate. Drizzle some flaxseed oil over the steamed broccoli and serve.

Steak with Creamy Mushroom Sauce, Sweet Potato Chips and Broccoli

Serves: 1

Ingredients

1 scotch fillet or porterhouse steak
2 tbsps olive oil (preferably extra virgin olive oil)
1 medium sweet potato, peeled and cut to resemble chips or cut lengthwise into wedges
1 cup broccoli, cut into florets
Drizzle of flaxseed oil
Salt and pepper, to taste

For mushroom cream sauce:
½ tsp olive oil (preferably extra virgin olive oil)
1 cup button mushrooms, sliced
⅓ cup fresh cream
½ tsp freshly ground black pepper or more, to taste
½ tsp salt

Instructions

Preheat fan-forced oven to 200°C (400°F). In a mixing bowl, toss sweet potato with 1 tbsp olive oil, salt and pepper. Transfer to a baking tray lined with a non-stick baking sheet and bake in the oven for about 20 minutes until cooked through, turning occasionally.

Meanwhile, heat the remaining olive oil in a frying pan over medium-high heat. Season the steak with some salt and pepper. Add steak to the frying pan and cook for about 3 minutes on each side or according to your preference. Remove from the pan and rest the steak covered at room temperature for at least 5 minutes.

Steam the broccoli. Put the broccoli florets into a steamer set over a pan of boiling water or if you don't have a steamer, put the broccoli florets in a pot and add a small amount of water so that the broccoli is only half covered. Cover the pot with a lid and place it on the stove and heat to medium high. Allow the broccoli to steam for about 5-10 minutes. The broccoli is finished steaming when it looks bright green and a fork slides into it easily.

Heat ½ tsp of olive oil in a saucepan over medium-high heat. Add the sliced mushrooms and stir-fry until they are lightly browned. Reduce the heat to medium. Then add cream, salt and pepper and bring to a boil. Reduce heat and cook for about 5-8 minutes, stirring occasionally.

Arrange the steak, sweet potato chips and broccoli on a plate. Pour the mushroom cream sauce of the steak, drizzle some flaxseed oil over the steamed broccoli and serve.

Steak with Roast Potatoes and Broccoli

Serves: 1

Ingredients

- 1 scotch fillet or porterhouse steak
- 2 tbsps olive oil (preferably extra virgin olive oil)
- 2 medium-sized potatoes (you can also use 1 medium-sized sweet potato instead), peeled and diced (about 1cm thick cubes)
- 1 cup broccoli, cut into florets
- Salt and pepper, to taste

Instructions

Preheat the oven to 230°C (450°F). Line a roasting pan with non-stick baking paper. Toss the potato cubes in about 1 tbsp of olive oil. Season with salt and pepper and spread in the pan. Roast for about 30 minutes.

Heat the remaining olive oil in a frying pan over medium-high heat. Season the steak with salt and pepper. Add steak to the frying pan and cook for about 3 minutes on each side or according to your preference. Remove from the pan and rest the steak at room temperature for at least 5 minutes.

Meanwhile, steam the broccoli. Put the broccoli florets into a steamer set over a pan of boiling water or if you don't have a steamer, put the broccoli florets in a pot and add a small amount of water so that the broccoli is only half covered. Cover the pot with a lid and place it on the stove and heat to medium high. Allow the broccoli to steam for about 5-10 minutes. The broccoli is finished steaming when it looks bright green and a fork slides into it easily.

Arrange the steak, roast potatoes and broccoli on a plate and serve.

Week 2: Drizzle some flaxseed oil over the steamed broccoli.

Desserts

Banana Cacao Overnight Chia Pudding
➔ *See Breakfast recipes*

Coconut Banana Muffins

Serves: 6

Ingredients

3 large eggs
¾ cup almond or coconut milk
2 tbsps coconut oil, melted
2 large bananas, mashed
½ cup coconut flour, sifted
½ tsp baking powder
½ tsp ground cinnamon – *optional*
½ cup walnuts, chopped – *optional*

Instructions

Preheat fan-forced oven to 180°C (350°F).

In a bowl, whisk together the eggs, milk, coconut oil, mashed banana and chopped walnuts (optional) until well combined. Then add the coconut flour, baking powder and cinnamon (optional) and whisk to combine.

Spoon the batter into a greased muffin tray and bake in the oven for about 25-30 minutes or until cooked through.

Raw Chocolate Mousse

Serves: 4

Ingredients

1 large avocado, skin and seed removed
1 banana
3 tbsps coconut oil, melted
4 tbsps raw cacao powder (unsweetened)
2 tbsps honey or maple syrup
⅛ tsp (approx. 2 pinches) sea salt

Instructions

Place all of the ingredients in a food processor and process until smooth. Then put the mousse into individual dishes and refrigerate for at least 1 hour before eating.

Sweet Potato Brownies

Ingredients

2 cups raw sweet potato, peeled and grated
½ cup butter or coconut oil, melted
½ cup honey or maple syrup
2 large eggs
2 tsps vanilla powder or paste
¼ - ½ cup raw cacao powder (unsweetened)
2 tsps baking powder
1 tsp bicarbonate of soda
2 tbsps coconut flour
½ cup walnuts – *optional*
½ cup raspberries, fresh or frozen – *optional*

Instructions

Preheat the oven to 180°C (350°F).

Combine the sweet potato, butter or coconut oil, honey (or maple syrup), eggs, vanilla and walnuts (optional) in a food processor or blender. Then add the cacao powder, baking powder and bicarbonate of soda to the food processor or blender and combine. Finally stir through the coconut flour. The batter should have a thick, cake batter-like consistency. If the batter seems a little wet, add a little bit more coconut flour.

Line a small slice tin with baking paper and pour the batter into the tin. Top with raspberries (optional).

Bake for about 25 minutes. The brownies are done when the centre is firm to touch and a skewer inserted comes out clean.

Let it cool before slicing.

Enjoy at room temperature or warm with double cream or coconut cream and some fresh berries!

You can store the brownies in an airtight container in the fridge.

Beverages

Chia Bubble Tea (Refreshing summer drink!)

Serves: 1

Ingredients

- 1 cup of Rooibos tea, chilled
- 1 tbsp raw cacao powder (unsweetened)
- 1 vanilla bean or 2 tsps vanilla extract
- 1 tbsp honey (or sweetener of choice)
- 2 tbsps almond milk (or milk of choice)
- 1 tbsp chia seeds

Instructions

Add the chia seeds to the chilled Rooibos tea and refrigerate overnight.

Combine the cacao powder, vanilla, honey and milk in a small bowl by whisking. Then add this mixture to the tea and stir well to combine. Serve chilled.

Coconut Milk Hot Chocolate with Cinnamon (Great winter warmer!)

Serves: 1

Ingredients

1 cup coconut milk (unsweetened)
1 tbsp raw cacao powder (unsweetened)
Pinch of cinnamon

Instructions

Pour the coconut milk, cacao powder and cinnamon into a saucepan. Stir and heat over medium heat until everything is well combined and heated through (but not boiling!).

Sauces

Soy Sauce Substitute

Makes: ⅔ cup

Ingredients

> 1 cup homemade or low sodium (or no salt added), no MSG added
> store-bought beef stock
> 2 tbsps balsamic vinegar
> 2 tsps cider vinegar
> 1 tbsp + 1 tsp molasses
> Pinches of white pepper, garlic powder and ground ginger
> Salt, to taste – *optional*

Instructions

Place all ingredients (except salt) in a small saucepan. Bring the mixture to a gentle simmer (small bubbles should just break on the surface), and let it simmer until it is reduced to about ⅔ cup. Season with salt, if you wish, or leave as a low-salt condiment. Pour into a tight-sealing jar and refrigerate (up to 10 days).

REFERENCES

Bartimeus, P. 2011. *Natural Wonderfoods*. London: Duncan Baird Publishers.

Cabot, S. 2009. *Help for Depression and Anxiety*. Camden, NSW: WHAS.

Davis, L. C. 2012. More Facts About Caffeine/Coffee – And Its Effect On The Body. *The New Zealand Journal of Natural Medicine*, (6).

Fassa, P. 2014. 16 Magnesium Deficiency Symptoms. *The New Zealand Journal of Natural Medicine*, (13).

Fiedler, C. 2009. *The Complete Idiot's Guide to Natural Remedies*. New York: Alpha Books.

Fone, H. 2008. *Emotional Freedom Technique for Dummies*. Chichester, West Sussex, England: John Wiley & Sons.

Fox, B. 2010. *Power over Panic*. Camberwell, Vic.: Penguin.

Hicks, J. and Hicks, J. 2011 *Healthy Eating, Healthy World*. Dallas, Tex.: BenBella Books, Inc.

Holford, P. 2012. *6 Weeks To Superhealth*. London: Piatkus.

McDermott, I. and Jago, W. 2001. *Brief NLP Therapy*. London: Sage Publications.

Merrell, W., Augustine, M. and Dowdle, H. 2013. *The Detox Prescription*. New York: Rodale Inc.

Muir, A. J. 2010. *Relaxation Techniques*. London: Teach Yourself.

NurrieStearns, M. and NurrieStearns, R. 2010. *Yoga for Anxiety*. Oakland, CA: New Harbinger Publications.

Plant, J. A. and Stephenson, J. 2008. *Beating Stress, Anxiety & Depression*. London: Piatkus.

Rama, Ballentine, R. and Hymes, A. 1998. *Science of Breath*. Honesdale, PA.: Himalayan Institute Press.

Tallis, F. 2009. *How to Stop Worrying*. London: Sheldon.

Whitten, H. 2009. *Cognitive Behavioural Coaching Techniques for Dummies*. Chichester, West Sussex: Wiley.

Wilson, S. 2012. *I Quit Sugar*. Sydney, N.S.W.: Pan Macmillan.

Wolfe, D. 2009. *Superfoods*. Berkeley: North Atlantic Books.

Wright, K. 2004. *Guide to Wellbeing*. London: Geddes and Grosset.

ABOUT THE AUTHOR

The author, Jacqueline Brandes, has suffered from anxiety for many years which has led her on a journey of finding ways to overcome anxiety naturally. She is a qualified Solomon Yogalates™ teacher (completed in 2009) and Iyengar Yoga teacher (completed in 2011). She is certified in Sports Nutrition (completed in 2011), Weight Loss (completed in 2011) and Healthy Eating for Weight Loss (completed in 2012). Jacqueline also completed further training in the following topics:

Training	Completed in
8 units of instruction in Foundation – Extremeties course in **Ortho-Bionomy®**	2010
"How To Get Unstuck" online training conducted by Susi Hately from Functional Synergy, Canada Included the following lessons: • Principles for "Getting Unstuck" • Hip and Pelvis Mechanics • Shoulder Mechanics • Shoulder and Hips Mechanics	2012
"The Wisdom of Jalandhara Bandha: Neck Health and Why It Matters" online course conducted by Doug Keller, Yoga U Online Trainings	2012
"Mapping the Body - Anatomy Trains for Yoga Practitioners" online course conducted by Tom Myers, Yoga U Online Trainings	2013
"Asana Practice Screen for Yoga Teachers" online course conducted by Chrys Kub, Yoga U Online Trainings	2013
"Freeing the Breath - Keys to Releasing and Retraining the Abdominals" online course conducted by Julie Gudmestad, Yoga U Online Trainings	2013

Training	Completed in
"Songs of the Spine - Yoga, Scoliosis and Spinal Health" online course conducted by Narelle Carter-Quinlan, Yoga U Online Trainings	2013
"Subtle Yoga: Enlivening the Healing Power of the Meridians in Yoga Asanas" online course conducted by Kristine Kaoverii Weber, Yoga U Online Trainings	2013
"Pelvic Balance - Dealing with Shifts, Tilts, Rotations and Their Effects" online course conducted by Doug Keller, Yoga U Online Trainings	2013
"Yoga for Back Pain: The Essential Guide to Lower Back Pain Relief" online course conducted by Robin Rothenberg, Yoga U Online Trainings	2014
"I Love Anatomy" online training conducted by Susi Hately from Functional Synergy, Canada	2014
"Yoga for Healthy Sleep: Keys to Overcoming Insomnia" online course conducted by Dr. Loren Fishman and Ellen Saltonstall, Yoga U Online Trainings	2014
"Issues in the Tissues - Releasing Emotional Holdings through Movement and Body Repatterning" online course conducted by Tom Myers, Yoga U Online Trainings	2014
"Yoga Techniques to Lift Your Mood: Simple Yoga Practices for Depression and Anxiety" online course conducted by Amy Weintraub, Yoga U Online Trainings	2014
"Yoga for Back Pain: Keys to Preventing and Healing Sacroiliac Instability" online course conducted by Robin Rothenberg, Yoga U Online Trainings	2015

Jacqueline's website jbyogafit.com offers online Yoga, Pilates and Yogalates classes.

CREDITS

Cover by Nada Orlic

CPSIA information can be obtained
at www.ICGtesting.com
Printed in the USA
BVOW09s1940251117

501251BV00023B/1154/P

9 781503 216020